HOME LIFE THREE

HOME LIFE
THREE

Alice Thomas Ellis

with illustrations by Zé

Duckworth

First published in 1988 by
Gerald Duckworth & Co. Ltd.
The Old Piano Factory
43 Gloucester Crescent, London NW1

The text of this book is
drawn from the 'Home Life' column
of the *Spectator*

ISBN 0 7156 2270 6

British Library Cataloguing in Publication Data
Ellis, Alice Thomas, *1932–*
  Home life three.
  I. Title
  828′.91409

  ISBN 0-7156-2270-6

Photoset in North Wales by
Derek Doyle & Associates, Mold, Clwyd.
Printed in Great Britain by
Billing & Sons Limited, Worcester

Contents

Contents

January

Glittering occasion

Well, after all the mutterings of 'humbug' and worse, the festivities passed off almost painlessly and a glittering occasion was enjoyed by nearly all. Except I forgot the Stilton, the port and the crackers, and I left the mince pies in the freezer together with the *vol-au-vents*, and the tangerines in the office. I don't care either. The mice can have them. And I didn't do one single left-over thing with the turkey. I threw the beastly creature's carcase away.

All the presents worked out nicely though. Some years ago when asked what I wanted for Christmas I said, 'Oh scent, ear-rings – anything', and ever since then that's what I've got. People can smell me coming for miles and if I had five ears on each side of my head it would take me weeks to display all my ear-rings. I should've said, 'Mink, oil wells, tiaras ...'

The fourth son was particularly impressed by the present from his sister. On the morning of the day, he was speaking to a friend on the telephone and expressing his desire for a white silk scarf to wear on his motorbike or in his aeroplane or somewhere. Wordlessly the daughter handed him a package from under the tree – and yes, that's right. He said it was the best coincidence since the time he was driving into the Mojave desert and remarked to his companion that his most favourite car was a 1962

Thunderbird convertible. As he spoke, there in the middle
of nowhere appeared a junk yard, and in it was – yes, that's
right. I never know whether I find coincidences more
reassuring or creepy. Evidence of an underlying pattern
or of a malevolent desire to tease on the part of some
Elemental.

Caroline forgot the crackers as well. She rang up when it
was all over and we comforted each other rather as the
survivors of a battle lie back, war-stained and weary in the
dug-out, sharing a fag. Her family also had a lovely time,
whereas she confessed that for a moment there it was her
darkest hour – plodding round the shops with a bagful of
dead ducks, etc., and wondering why the Christma. tree
lights didn't work. I don't quite know why the whole thing
is so much agony, but it seems to get more of a damn
nuisance every year, until you finally sit down at the table
and there's only the clearing up left to face.

There was a record crop of murders this year too. Beryl
tried to strangle me on Christmas Eve, but she apologised
very nicely and explained that she hadn't got me in mind
at the time, only she couldn't get at the person she really
wanted to kill. I didn't care, feeling just then that a
murderer would be doing me a favour. Anyway she's very
slight and didn't even rumple my black velvet, and her
presents were wonderful – a cigarette case *en suite* with a
lighter for me – so I shan't stop smoking for yet awhile.
She gave me a book of ghost stories as well to save me
having to watch telly all the time, *and* a picture of St Joseph
and Our Lady with Our Lord as a lad with long hair. Fairly
comprehensive, you must agree.

The black velvet got off very lightly considering the
fraught nature of the season. I had just wit enough left not
to wear it while wrestling with the turkey and wore a lacy
cream-coloured thing instead. Sure enough it ended up

9

richly spattered in gravy, but Janet soaked it in some magical solution and it's all right now. Alfred turned up to do the housework despite a hangover, and apart from kicking Cadders for dossing on one of the drawing-room chairs while he was hoovering, he behaved very well, considering.

We have about twelve bags of empty bottles and various festering detritus but when the bin men come all evidence of the occasion will have been wiped out.

Except for the tree. It is still sitting balefully in a corner, winking its horrible little lights and flashing its tawdry tinsel, and it needn't think it's going to last until Twelfth Night. I'm going to strip it and throw it off the balcony and chop it up in a million bits, and next year I think I may spend Christmas in Saudi Arabia.

Lost cause

A long time ago when I was too young to know better I went beagling on a snowy day and got stuck with a girl whose name, as far as I remember, was Mary Bedstead, and a perfectly stupid hound called Venus. Venus had to be lifted over fences and carried across ditches. Lord knows where the hare and everyone else got to but I don't recall seeing any of them ever again. In the course of time me and Miss Bedstead and Venus staggered back to base, frozen, exhausted and deeply fed up with each other.

Serve us right. I've never had all that much faith in canine sagacity and now two of the silly brutes have got themselves lost up the mountain behind the house. (We're in Wales, not Camden Town.) Some chap took them hunting for foxes and they got separated. The hounds are howling and the chap is bellowing all over the valley and I came here for a spot of peace and quiet. The little girls are distressed at the thought of the poor little lost dogs (what about the poor little harassed foxes?) and have gone out to look for them. If I have to turn out and look for two little lost girls as a consequence of this I shall head straight back to London and the riots. There's a heavy frost outside and a fairly heavy one inside, come to think of it. It could be another world. Only yesterday I was running round

11

Camden Town in sandals and no socks and now I'm huddled over a big fire as close as Shadrach, Meshach and Abednego. I'm not complaining. I made a New Year resolution to stop swearing and complaining, because I was beginning to find myself tedious, and people had started avoiding me. It's an awful old vale of tears but one must grit the teeth and soldier on, I suppose.

I wonder what happened to the guest who set off yesterday to come and stay with us. One of her friends just telephoned and told us that that's what she'd done, but she isn't here. I've looked. Sometimes there are so many people around that one more could pass unnoticed, but not at the moment. Only four of us and all unmistakable, especially Janet who looks like an Abominable Something in about fourteen layers and moon boots. The guest was bringing two Pekineses with her as well and they would certainly not have gone unnoticed – unless they'd whipped up the mountain to look for foxes with the other dopey hounds. Everything is so worrying. Perhaps, I think, dementedly, the guest went up the mountain looking for foxes. It would be out of character, but then life is full of surprises.

Night is beginning to fall and the stars to glitter. The hounds have stopped howling. Is this, I ask myself, because they've eaten the guest? Oh no, surely not. The huntsman has assured the little girls that they are gentle as lambs, affectionate and totally harmless – except, of course, to foxes – and that if they turn up at the house we need feel no fear. And their names are Tanya and Sprocket. As if I cared. The only fear I feel at the moment is that of having to go out in ten below looking for little girls (and the guest) who are looking for hounds who are looking for foxes. I really don't want to have to do that. I'd rather sit by the fire and see pictures in it. No, that's no

good. All I can see is mountains and foxes and missing guests. This is a great start to the New Year. Is there any point in having hysterics when there's no one to watch? Janet has taken another departing guest to the station along the icy roads. Will I ever see Janet again? Will she inadvertently run over the guest, who I now picture rushing suddenly out of the hedgerow flapping her arms, pursued by a pack of hounds and some vengeful foxes? I think I'll spend 1987 in a rest home.

The little girls, at least, have just returned so I'll go and beat them to a pulp for frightening me, and then I'll have a stiff vodka, and probably swear a bit.

So much for New Year resolutions. I blame the foxes.

Blue flu news

I don't believe it. The Blue Flu's back. I forgot about it for a while, having been suffering intermittently since just after Christmas. I caught it off guard a week or so ago. While, as it were, it wasn't looking, I gave it a good push and slammed the door on it. Always slow to learn, I assumed that that was the end of the matter, forgetting that previously it has often slipped out for a moment and has always come back. This time it took a little longer, but it was only hiding round the corner and now it's got its feet firmly under the table again. I think it's taken some sort of vow and is never going to leave me.

The sickening thing is it's all my own fault. Wandering along a country lane in the rain and the hail and the sleet as Christmas receded, I remarked complacently to Janet that I was *never* ill. I usually know better than to do this but I wasn't thinking. I did hastily touch a sort of gnarled bark but it was clearly the wrong sort of wood, and too late anyway since already some nosey-parker pagan spirit had overheard me and gone rushing off to his heathen boss gods pointing and crying excitedly, 'There's a lady down there in that lane committing hubris.' Nemesis was round in no time. Would that the telephone engineers were so prompt. I was talking to Deirdre the other evening when the telephone's pagan spirit decided that we'd said enough and cut us off. He resolutely refused to allow us to converse all that night and the next day. Eventually the telephone man arrived and said that her telephone had simply worn out, but I think that was because interfering pagan spirits had been plaguing it for longer than it could stand, not because it found Deirdre and me boring.

I wonder if our Editor is quite well. We lunched together last week when the flu must have been tiptoeing back to me, and I have no reason to suppose that it does not add promiscuity to its other loathsome characteristics. We both got our hair wet too. It was raining so we walked to the restaurant and when we arrived and sat down we, as one, and without consultation, dried our hair with our table napkins. Luckily they were the cloth sort. Shortly afterwards I saw a bit of a programme about an American School of Manners which seems to have moved over here, and the lady teacher was telling some rather sceptical-looking English kiddies that they must fold their hands in their laps to stop their napkins falling on the floor. I suppose when they were actually wielding their knives and forks ('Remember, girls and boys, always start on the

15

outside and then you can't go wrong') they would be permitted to leave the napery to its own devices, but I can't quite picture the expression on teacher's face if they started putting it on their heads.

I was reminded of the last time I thought I'd evicted the flu. The pipes were frozen and life generally unappealing, so I volunteered to take the family to our newest local Chinese restaurant. At the conclusion of the meal, round came the hot damp flannels, and I wondered what the reaction would be if I should encourage the family to seize the opportunity to strip off and have a quick rub down, since bathing would be out of the question until the spring thaw. I like these little restaurantial bonuses, like free kir and garlic prawns at one end and chocolates or turkish delight at the other, and more coffee after the bill has been paid. I don't suppose they're really all that free but as they're not written down on the bill they *feel* free.

I suppose if I'm going to have this infernal flu for ever I'm going to have to learn to live with it. This will mean that I would be more sensible to go to down-market caffs with tomato ketchup free on each table and a glass containing folded paper napkins. I mean it would be too awful, and going altogether too far, to blow one's nose in a linen napkin. Oh God. Atishooo.

Forgotten grains

'What was Elizabeth Barrett Browning's dog called?' asked Janet, *apropos* of not much.

Now of course I knew perfectly well what the animal was called, but faced with a direct question my mind goes blank, which is why you've never seen me on Mastermind.

'Damn,' I said, 'if you hadn't asked me I would have told you – it begins with F. Fancy? Fanny? Fishy?'

'No,' said Janet, concentrating deeply, 'It's a silly name. Something like Toilet.'

I said nobody had ever called a dog Toilet – not even the Barretts of Wimpole St., but she insisted it was something like that. Imagine, I invited her, running round the park calling 'Toilet, Toilet!'

But she said she *knew* it was *something* like that and went about with her eyes crossed and her brow furrowed until she gave a sudden triumphant scream. 'Flush,' she cried.

This was at the height of the great freeze when the lavatories didn't, so there may be a Freudian explanation for our loss of memory. I have now forgotten the posh word for loss of memory, so I'm going to ask Janet. 'Amnesia,' she says without a moment's hesitation, so she's all right. How *could* I forget the word for loss of memory?

Leafing through the *Psychopathology of Everyday Life* I learn that ladies who are unable to have children

17

'that's why I lie on the sofa, Mr Browning'

invariably read the word 'Stocks' as 'Storks'. I never had
that problem, so I don't know; although I don't quite see
why ladies who are always having babies don't also read
Storks for Stocks and shudder. It could work both ways,
couldn't it? Now would some great brain explain why I
always read Cat Pack for Car Park. Is this evidence of a
quirk in my sexual identity? Everybody always reads
Shoplifters for Shopfitters which is clearly evidence for
original sin, but why do I imagine Mr Isaacs is called Mr
Ice Axe, and why is Beryl worried because she thinks she
was rude to a person called Lord Broomcupboard? I tell
her there *is* no such person so she can't have offended
him, but she is very definite about it.

It isn't just the ravages of time that scramble the little
grey cells, because a million years ago when I was working
in a delicatessen somebody came in intent on purchasing a
tin of processed meat. 'A tin of Unox, please,' he said, this
being the brand name of the desired product. I stared at
him speechlessly, filled with a wild surmise. 'Eunuch's
what?' was the unspoken question lurking just behind my
teeth. I'll allow the Freudians that one.

Come to think of it, Beryl has created havoc in my social
life. She has twisted the names of so many people that I
simply do not dare introduce anyone to anyone for fear of
getting it wrong, and I have to fall back on 'You do know
each other, don't you?' or 'I'll just leave you to introduce
yourselves.' If I was even nastier than I am, I would say,
'Now, I'll just leave Beryl to introduce you', and stand back
and watch.

I am glad Flush was only a dog. It would be too terrible
if one had an acquaintance called – say – Hermione Flush,
and one announced her as Miss Toilet. Nor can Janet be
trusted in this regard. There is an advert on a wall round
the corner saying 'Brick makes Britain Beautiful', and

Janet doesn't read it like that. Was it Fluellen who pronounced his B's as P's? I think that's one more to the Freudians. On a purer level she has invented a splendid new character with his own fleet of personalised motors – the famous Flemish painter Hertz van Rental. She has just made me a cup of coffee and reminded me of something else that I always forget. I cannot remember how much sugar I take in coffee. I know to a grain how much I take in tea but not in coffee. I have a vision of myself breakfasting in a respectable hotel and asking my husband of many years how much sugar I take. I don't think even the Freudians could make anything of that.

February

Entertaining in style

This is the armpit of the year: dank, dark and unwholesome. Today there was a bit of thin watery sunlight and I foolishly imagined I was well enough to go shopping. I tottered home physically and emotionally exhausted with a box of mussels in garlic butter. I think it is in *The Pumpkin Eater* that a lady embarks on a nervous breakdown by bursting into tears in Harrods. I do it in Marks and Spencer's which is a touch down-market, but Harrods is too far. I had to lie down when I got back. Patrice is also afflicted. She had to go and buy food for Gloria and Jasper, her dogs, and the first thing she saw as she dragged her ailing form to the dog-meat shop was another dog who had been run over. In her state of health it was the final straw, and she addressed our Maker as follows: 'Right, you old Slacker up there, that's it. You're obviously looking the other way and I'm off.' The suicidal aspect of the illness was uppermost. I tried to reassure her by describing my own exactly similar symptoms, but our conversation was not a cheerful one. I wish I'd thought of suggesting that she'd merely stayed at home and rung Lord Avebury.

I am absolutely fed up with the whole business of food and cookery. The last thing I prepared was a horrible Chilli-con-Carne on Sunday. So many tins of stuff go into this dish that one always makes too much and nobody likes it anyway. I tried to give it to the cats, but they didn't fancy it at all. The tin opener broke on a tin of cat food the other day and I haven't been strong enough to buy another one so I expect we shall all starve to death, if the flu doesn't finish us off.

Nigella was so *right* in her piece of January 3rd. For those of you who haven't been listening, she spoke of a book called *Entertaining in Style* by Prue Leith and Polly Tyler, which was full of hair-raising notions such as 'Bistro Nights for Twenty' and 'Punk Parties for Forty' with amazing tips on how to drive yourself mad arranging the decor – never mind the food. She said it would make the authors of *Darling You Shouldn't Have Gone To So Much Trouble* take to their beds for weeks.

Now Caroline and I are the said authors of this masterly work (a sort of cheat-and-slut's handbook) and if we'd seen *Entertaining in Style* and if we hadn't already been laid low, I can state categorically that that is precisely the effect it would have had on us. We had always thought that *Entertaining with Elizabeth Craig* (1933) was the ultimate in exhausting suggestions. Her Heather Tea for instance: 'Go out and rob the common of its purple glory ... then hold your party indoors under a chandelier hidden in a shower bouquet of heather, tied in place with tartan ribbon.' It goes on and on and on with 'heather-coloured china and napkins and note-paper and Scotch buns and three sorts of tea and sandwiches and ices and rolled bread and butter with curls of young cress peeping out at each end ...' and the mere thought of it makes me feel ill.

I'm going to go and lie down again and if anyone wants anything to eat they can go and ask Prue Leith or Polly Tyler.

Bad form

I hate forms. I hate them with a simple, pure and dedicated passion, religious in its intensity. I don't understand them for a start, which is frequently an element in this type of mindless loathing. I am surrounded by tax forms, insurance forms and PLR. If they weren't going to give us money we wouldn't have to fill in forms. I wish they'd never thought of anything. I wish I were a Visigoth.

I had vowed not to watch the news or read the papers because all we ever get is the bad news, and who needs it, but faced with the forms I turned to the papers and was momentarily diverted by an item about two women who ran a brothel at their health studio while receiving £40 a week each from the Manpower Services Commission (I wonder how many forms they had to fill in?). Mrs Payne makes me smile too. Naturally I don't approve of all that sort of thing, but she isn't half funny. I don't quite see what distress she causes with her parties. It is as nothing to the alarm and despondency occasioned by the devious and evil monsters who afflict us with forms. I'd like to see them all in the dock or, even better, on the rack. They are guilty of the mental equivalent of GBH and have reduced me to a wreck: a racked wreck in dry dock.

I always used to listen to *The Archers* when in need of

reassurance and comfort, but most of the characters seem to have undergone frontal lobotomies and changed personality and I find it hard to recognise them. I am especially worried by Jennifer who used to be a *writer* – novels and columns. She is now a whining shadow of her former self: in fact, on due reflection, she bears absolutely no relation to her former self and perhaps should be sectioned. I think the rot started when she insisted on buying new garden furniture (a bad sign), and she has continued to deteriorate to the point where she wants Betty, the hired help, to wait at table because it disconcerts the guests if the hostess has to leap up and down. She is useless on the farm and expects everyone to run round after her. Her voice has gone up a register, she thinks of nothing but holidays and keeping up appearances, and hasn't done a stroke of work of any sort for months.

I have my own theory about what happened to her. I think Brian secretly suggested that she should look after the paperwork – her being a novelist and a journalist and all, and supposedly at home with that sort of thing – and it sent her demented. The final straw came, not from the farmyard, but from the PLR. She probably thought it was a terrorist organisation. Whatever the cause, she is now a vegetable and a horrible warning to those of us who used to write.

Perhaps I should listen to Capital Radio. A friend of the eldest son heard a story the other day about somebody who went into a jewellers' shop to buy a crucifix on a chain and the assistant asked if he wanted a plain cross or one with the little man on it. I find this extraordinary in view of something else I read in the newspapers. A US-based fundamentalist missionary sect has gone all the way to Paraguay to harass the Indian nomads in order to save their souls and has whisked off 24 of them to civilisation, where they have promptly contracted influenza to which they have no resistance. Now, I have resistance to influenza or I would have died yesterday. I also know who it is on the cross, and furthermore that he would not permit the souls of the Indians to suffer perpetual torment just because they wouldn't listen to the Mennonites (who sound to me like a sort of fossil shellfish) and in view of all this I ask myself why this sect doesn't leave the Indians in peace and come here with their influenza to educate the assistants in jewellers' shops? They could also have a word with Jennifer and remonstrate with the compilers of forms and the ladies from the health studio. Just as long as they leave Mrs Payne and me alone.

Curate's eggs

Just before I woke up this morning I was thinking in my sleep. What I was thinking was that February is like a strip of damp drugget laid in a narrow aisle, and one is oneself like a hard-boiled egg being pushed along by the toe of the curate. Someone awakened me with a cup of tea in time for me to grab the edges of this curious reflection and scrutinise it closely. Discount the Freudian connotations. What it means is that February is a nothing month, a means only to arriving in a (we hope) more clement season: the altar of May, we could say if we wished to wax poetic. I don't know what the curate was doing there, except that somewhere in the English unconscious the curate and the egg are inseparable. I wish I could remember all my dreams. Some of them are much more interesting than waking home life, and I could have sat before a sheet of blank white paper all day before I conceived of myself as a hard-boiled egg.

Home life at present is rather dull. Three of the sons are away, the boa constrictor has gone back to the pet-shop until her owner returns because I was not prepared to give her her dinner or clean up her tank, Janet has the influenza, the daughter is here only at weekends, and that leaves Someone, the eldest son, two cats and me. And a lot of moths. I don't know why I said 'dull'. The absence of all these people means I have no excuse for not spring-cleaning the entire house and squirting moth-killer in every neglected corner. The fact that I would rather die than do this is immaterial. Tidying up is not dull: exhausting, depressing, and frequently heart-breaking as one comes across the belongings of the dead, but never dull. Janet says throwing things away is very rewarding, but I don't find it so. The minute I consign something to the dustbin I find an urgent need for it. On the other hand, when the place is actually overflowing with junk, steps have to be taken.

There are areas in this house where it is impossible to take a step at all, unless it is upwards to the top of a pile of books. Alfie is going to have to be very firm and chuck things out without telling me. There is absolutely no need for me to retain the three discoloured, 30-year-old dress shirts and Someone's outgrown tennis shorts which came to light the other day at the bottom of a drawer. No, I tell myself, the V & A doesn't want them. Nobody wants them. Nor the candlewick counterpane with a big hole in it. And

there is no reason for me to keep the decayed red canvas sandals that I was once so fond of. They have gone crispy and are now unwearable. The lidless teapot is useless. I am never going to find a lid to fit it, or use it to grow bulbs in, and the poor don't need it any more than I do. Nor does anyone want the fifty odd socks tied in a bundle behind the washing machine. Nor the Mary Quant riding mac which has also gone crispy and keeps out not one solitary drop of rain. I am never going to tear out and use the blank pages of the children's old schoolbooks, and I don't need out-dated telephone directories to light fires. We only light the fire here on high days and holidays, and there are always piles of newspapers two feet deep which serve the purpose perfectly well. I must persuade Someone to sling out the million ties which he never wears – no, hang on – they could perhaps be used to mend the Victorian patchwork quilt which has some patches missing. Is this a sensible, thrifty idea or merely an extension of the neurosis?

The one thing we are short of here is ash-trays.

Someone uses pudding bowls for his cigar ends, which I find annoying. Alfie's brother-in-law who was a Wapping striker for ages has given me his favourite one because it bears an image of my church in Wales. I am not altogether cognisant of the rights and wrongs of the dispute but, as Alfie says, not all the strikers were brick-hurling monsters. His brother-in-law, for one, is an angel. Thank you, John. Whatever else gets thrown away, my Melangell ash-tray will always retain pride of place. I once kept a hard-boiled, dyed Easter egg in Wales for four years but a desperate mouse ate it, together with a plastic bottle of Tipp-Ex.

In the firing line

The telephone just rang and somebody who had, indeed, the correct number asked Janet if she was the Spanish Consulate. She denied it. I am fed up with the telephone. For some remote reason the last engineer to come and fiddle with the thing put, in the kitchen which is where we most usually answer it, a hand-set with a sort of deaf aid on it. Some of us are short-sighted and Janet has a crick in her neck but not one of us is in the slightest degree deaf. This miracle of modern science has to be constantly adjusted as you speak, since sometimes the person on the other end is unaudible and sometimes his voice comes roaring out with the force of a water cannon.

The telephone also has a curious effect on Puss. She is

not an unusually affectionate cat, but when one is speaking on the telephone she springs up and sits on it, turning herself round the cord, purring loudly and dribbling and patting one's face with her paw, claws unretracted. 'Oh sod off you stupid mog,' one mutters, and the person on the other end takes offence. I've grown tired of explaining.

Patrice rang to say she had suffered another dog episode. She is dogged at the moment by dog episodes. Walking abroad one day she saw a puppy playing chicken in the main road while its owner stood helplessly on the pavement and the cars whizzed by. Dauntlessly Patrice leapt forward and, heedless of the danger flew to and fro until she had collared the creature. She explained to its owner, a foreigner, that it was inadvisable to let so young an animal roam at large and he shouted at her. Sometimes the stupidity and the cruelty of the world really gets to Patrice. She asked me whom she could sue for being born, and I couldn't think of anyone. I want to sue somebody about the telephone. Janet spent hours the other day trying to get through to the Arts Educational Trust. No answer, no ringing tone, no nothing. So she rang Directory Enquiries, and they were engaged. Then she rang 100, and no one answered. Alfie applied for a telephone a long time ago. He bought the actual object himself from a shop and then asked them to come and bring him a line so he could plug it in and use it, but they said they were on strike, so he's keeping it as an ornament until they decide to up tools again.

I don't know which I find more tiresome, the telephone or the post. I keep getting letters which I really should answer, but I hate answering letters even more than I hate answering the telephone. Perhaps I should keep carrier pigeons. People write to tick me off – more in sorrow than in anger, I hasten to add, and always very nicely, but half the time they've missed the point, which is annoying. I *know* I smoke too much and I *will* give it up one day, but I don't care a bit if I don't live to be 103, and I don't get short of breath if I run for a train. I am truly sorry for the man whose lover died of AIDS, but I never even hinted that Heaven had it in for the love that dare not speak its name. I said that some of the practices I had learned of since AIDS hit the headlines sounded highly peculiar. And they do. And I never said I thought Mrs Payne was a good thing. I don't. I said I thought she was jolly funny. And she is. Ages ago I wrote somewhere that I was going to worry more about the daughter when it came to sex than I had about the sons. I wasn't thinking about disease at the time. I'd remembered that females get pregnant; and some fatuous person wrote to accuse me of something. I don't know quite what it was, but I think she was having a sort of internal conflict with herself and I had inadvertently stepped in the firing line. I found her wildly irritating.

I've got to stop now because the telephone is ringing. I bet there's a letter on the mat too.

March

Holier than thou

We spent the weekend at the seaside with an old friend – a medical man. He told us at one point, with quiet pride that he had just brought one of his patients back from the Brink of Death. I thought about this for a while and then I told him that if by chance he should ever discover me lying around on the brink of death I'd thank him to leave me there. I did not at all care for the sound of the condition of the grateful patient. Caroline and I have made a pact that, if one of us should find herself incarcerated in a caring institution surrounded by idiots officiously striving to keep us alive, the other will whizz in with a wheelchair and whip her away. Plus all the morphine necessary of course.

Many sorts of professional men cause the hackles to rise. I suppose the tax-man heads the list. I have only recently come, as it were, eyeball to eyeball with this person and I hate him. Previously he bled my money away at source by stealth, but now I am called self-employed and I have to *give* it to him – in the sure and certain knowledge that the silly bugger is going to spend it on torpedoes. I heard the other day that *one* torpedo costs a million pounds. I can't think how the rest of you have been tolerating him all this time. Next comes the Bank Manager. I hate him too. I'm sure I don't have to explain why. Bank managers are a separate species like zebras and differ very little each from

'Most judges only ever meet other judges socially.'

the other. Lawyers are detestable, with judges in a special category. Judges are distinguished by such asinine arrogance, such invincible ignorance of the ordinary ways of the world that the non-judge can only flop around like a flounder gasping in disbelief at the way they carry on. Did you know that most judges only ever meet other judges socially? I suppose no one else could stand them. Architects are arrogant too. Like most of the rest of the population I should like to round them up and make them live in a tower block. For ever. When you see what they've done to our cities for ever is not long enough. Politicians – ugh.

I suppose dentists and opticians and vicars do less harm than good, but they're all too busy for my taste – 'What *have* you been doing to your teeth – eyes – soul ...?' Caroline finds homeopaths the worst. They clutch your pulse, roll their eyes heavenwards and enquire how on earth you got your liver into that state. The answer is obvious, so why ask the question? Homeopaths, being so pure themselves, just enjoy disapproving of other people.

Which brings me back to our friend of the weekend. He greatly disapproves of smoking, so naturally I smoked like a nuclear reactor all the first evening. I smoked so much I poisoned myself and the next day decided that I never wanted to *see* another cigarette ever again. He was very pleased at this and when I started coughing my head off explained that this was usual, because my lungs had been anaesthetised by smoke and now were beginning to feel again. He painted a most moving picture of the poor things, but instead of feeling compassionate towards them I felt a wave of the purest sadism. How dare the stupid things be so *wet*. You just wait – I told them – Carrera y Carrera for you, as soon as I'm better.

I'm afraid I had a rather similar feeling about the old in

the cold when Mrs Thatcher and Mr Kinnock were madly trying to outdo each other in the matter of who loved the old best, and who minded most if they all froze to death. Oooh. The hypocrisy of it made me grind my teeth so much I almost had to visit the dentist. That's the trouble with the *bien pensant* – rather than resemble them in any degree one rushes to the other extreme and finds oneself announcing that one is really, upon due consideration, actually rather in favour of bunging grandpa in the frigidaire.

This same dreadful perversity drove me straight to the off-licence the moment we returned, where I bought a packet of 20 and proceeded to demolish the lot. I've poisoned myself again and have given up smoking, but if anyone starts to treat me like a convert entering the fold I hereby give him notice that I shall take to smoking a Meerschaum. So shut up.

Toad away

Poor Janet's toad, Michael, passed away the other day and she was very upset. Don't give your heart to a toad to tear. Now her fish have got white spot – a fell disease – and she has discovered 13 of them floating belly upward. She took the survivors in a Tupperware container to a fish expert and he shook his head gravely, giving her a bright blue substance to put in their water, but not holding out much hope.

March

I've been reading Herodotus and for some reason this reminds me of the chap who was blinded by the Gods for throwing his spear at the Nile in a rage. They said he could be cured by applying the urine of a woman who had slept only with her husband. He tried his own wife's first and it didn't work. Oh *Lord*. Picture the scene. He tried absolutely umpteen ladies before he found the one who proved efficacious. He married her (don't know what he did with her husband, poor fellow) and put all the others, wife included, in a place called Red Clod and burnt them to a crisp.

This deplorable tale reminded me in turn of a certain part of this country where for some other reason many families had to have blood tests and it was found that most of the daddies could not in fact have fathered their putative kiddies. Talk yourself out of that one, Nefertiti, Mrs Smith ... how human nature does not seem to change.

The Egyptians used to shave their eyebrows off when their cats died, and all of themselves, including their heads, when their dogs died. Cats were embalmed and buried in sacred receptacles in Bubastis, dogs were buried in sacred burial places in their own town, and so were weazels. Fieldmice and hawks, forsooth, were taken to Buto and ibises to Hermopolis. Bears and wolves were buried wherever they chanced to be discovered lying dead. We know the Egyptians were nuts about burying things, but to go all the way to Buto – wherever that may be, but its bound to be a long way from somewhere – carting a deceased fieldmouse, seems to me excessive.

Perhaps Herodotus got it wrong, or perhaps the natives were telling him fibs. I was informed in Alexandria that Alexander the Great had, with his own hands, presented the mosque with its magnificent chandelier. On the other

38

hand I remember taking a ruined teddy bear all the way to Wales in a shoe box to be buried under a tree, and many the hamsters and fallen fledglings who have been despatched with due ceremony by my weeping children, so perhaps this is only another, largely forgotten, aspect of human nature. Tobias the Elder was always compulsively burying people when the King had expressedly told him he wasn't to.

I asked Janet, in view of all this, how she disposed of her spotty fish, and she said she had stood to attention by the loo, singing the Last Post. I don't think she need have gone so far as embalming them, but this does seem a little casual – though then again perhaps a watery grave is suitable to a dead fish. She hardly dares go home and look in the tank because home is beginning to remind her of a necropolis. Her cats are always carrying in rats – alive and dead – and I must ask her if they bring in fieldmice. I never made it as far as Upper Egypt, and if Buto should chance to be round there we could hop on a plane and go and bury them.

She is particularly worried about Sybil, her catfish who has grown to a great size and mainly eats – of all things – cat food. I don't think Sybil sounds like a very nice fish since she also ate her mate Bruno. One day he was there, said Janet, and the next he wasn't. Not a whisker, not a sign of him. She peered under the stones and even examined the surrounding carpet in case he'd leapt out, but Bruno had completely disappeared and only one possible conclusion could be arrived at. Perhaps Sybil thought he'd been sleeping with other catfish. If you're only a catfish it is perhaps no more reprehensible to eat your unfaithful husband than it is as an ancient Egyptian to burn your faithless wife, and at least she only ate the one. The interfering Pheros, after all, burnt dozens of other people's wives as well. Perhaps Bruno *was* Pheros passing through the fish course of his reincarnations. What a cheering thought.

Paper mountain

I have just cleared up another pile of papers. Well, almost. Whereas they were in one teetering heap at the far end of the kitchen table, now they're in a number of smaller heaps all over the kitchen table.

Unanswered letters – which are going to stay that way because I never answer letters and it's probably the guilt occasioned by this that causes me to wake, sweating, in the small hours – constitute the largest pile. I'm not going to throw them away. I'm going to put them in a big envelope addressed to posterity, and after a while it won't matter that I haven't answered them; except of course for those associated with gas, electricity, tax, etc., and the people who sent them will undoubtedly write again – so it doesn't matter what I do with them either. Invitations are more worrying, since they really do demand a response and my instinctive response to suggestions that I go places and do things, especially in the evening, is not friendly. In a way I'm grateful to the Post Office for being so unreliable because one can always claim not to have received any mail.

One of the letters is from an Earl inviting me to buy a bit of his castle on a time-share basis and to whizz off for the weekend and have a look. 'This,' he writes, 'is no crumbling, draughty, ancient keep.' It's luxurious with swimming pools and adventure playgrounds and it sounds the purest hell. I like draughty, crumbling old ruins. Makes me feel at home. Our AIDS warning has come to light together with *The Sun/News of the World* Bingo leaflet and reminds me of the extraordinary turn everyone's conversation has taken. I don't know anyone who a few years ago would have discussed the inadvisability of anal intercourse at lunch. For some reason I have a Masonic leaflet and not the remotest idea where it came from. It suggests halfway through that since gauntlets are seldom worn and are probably mouldering away in drawers they should be sewn up at the narrow end and used to collect the alms. What a good wheeze.

Now I find a splendid leaflet giving 62 reasons for the naffness of the New Mass. Did you know that six Protestant ministers collaborated in making it up? I knew it, I knew it! I was never a very good Catholic and now I'm an absolutely lousy one because whenever I do force myself to Mass I find it impossible to feel religious since its ugliness makes me irritable. I don't mind Protestantism if it keeps itself to itself but I don't want to be one. If I did I would. And I *won't* shake hypocritical hands with a load of smelly strangers, God forgive me. I go to church for the sake of the Lord and if I feel like shaking hands with people I'll do it in my own good time. You can see that this New Mass idiocy has made me not only a worse Catholic but a worse human being. I'll probably have to put in extra time in Purgatory. It isn't fair. I see in today's paper that some stupid nun says there is no scriptural basis for opposing the ordination of women. Oh yes there is. I understand why men are getting so sullen and resentful. It looks as though bossy womankind won't trust them to do anything by themselves.

There's a copy of Agatha Christie's *After the Funeral* lurking under several magazines and MSS so I'll read that this afternoon and calm myself down, and when I've done that I'll read *Maxims and Examples of the Saints* which Andrew gave me on Saturday. And when I've done that I'll put my mind to the problem of why I've got a bit of paper bearing the address of Tariq Ali tucked under an ex-apple in the fruit bowl. If anybody's got any ideas I'd rather they didn't write and tell me. I prefer to figure it out for myself.

Good red meat

Animals and their diets keep forcing themselves on my attention. There was a dog in the garden the other day, eating the garbage. He left carrying an empty tin of catfood: small reward for all the rummaging he'd been doing, but dogs don't like swede peelings or biscuit packets. This fact was reinforced by a man on the wireless the other day who had been approached by a born-again vegetarian asking how she could convert her dog to her views in order to help him to Higher Things. I don't see how she can. Dogs are carnivorous and their systems cannot, I imagine, sustain themselves on lettuce and lentils. Even Bernard Shaw after some years of vegetarianism had to have injections of liver extract or something disgusting because he'd grown anaemic; and the human frame *can* adjust to a meatless diet. Mine has, more or less, but this is not because of conviction. I can't be bothered with butcher's meat – either buying it or cooking it. Something in the pasta line is about all I can cope with at the moment, although I do buy very little steaks for the adolescents. Adolescents, like dogs, need meat. So do cats. Cats are even more carnivorous than dogs or adolescents – or foxes. Foxes can keep body and soul together on earthworms and the contents of suburban bins, but cats need red meat. One of our cats has a passion for olives but he couldn't actually live on them. He treats them rather as human beings do – as an appetizer – except that human beings don't go down on all fours to chase the pip around when they've eaten the rest of it. Not if they're sober they don't.

Puss and Cadders eat tin after tin of vile-smelling cat food – rabbit-, chicken-, liver- or beef-flavoured. But rabbit-, chicken-, liver- or beef-flavoured *what*? I used to fear that it might be whale meat, and suffer pangs of guilt. Whales are quite as beautiful and beguiling as cats – in their own way – and I don't like the idea of the one eating the other. Now I think whaling is largely out of style in this country and I suspect that the cats are currently consuming horse meat. This is also upsetting, since horses are not really bred for food. They put in years of work of one sort or another and it seems deeply unfair that after all that they should then be slaughtered and tinned. Cows, pigs, sheep and chickens are not expected to run races or go pony-trekking before they turn up in the abattoir. I do not care to dwell on their lives and eventual deaths either, but at least they are not brought up to expect anything different. Horses have always had a lousy deal, carrying people into battle, pulling carts and jumping over barbed-wire fences, whereas cats have been pampered and cossetted all through the ages, and hardly ever expected to do a stroke of work apart from catching rats and mice, which is in their own interests anyway if there aren't any tins of horse meat around. They catch birds too, which is wicked but clever of them. Have you ever tried to catch a healthy bird with its wits about it? Janet's Cesare unwrapped one in her dining-room the other day. Not a pretty sight, but you can't argue with a cat. I've tried and I know. They stare at you balefully and go away and wash their whiskers, wearing an air of contempt. Then when it's dinner time they jump on the shelf and kick a tin of cat food into the vegetable crock just to let you know what is expected of you. I don't altogether approve of their characters, but they've been well and truly spoiled for centuries and it's too late to do anything about it now.

April

Mouse sense

It occurred to me the other day that when a person implores you to be reasonable what he means is that you should speed round forthwith to his point of view. We are having bits of the home repainted. Not before time. Only this week a chap was discovered in the garden, lying down taking photographs of the frontage. When we enquired why, he said he was looking for a location for a film on Channel 4. Channel 4, mark you. Not BBC1 or 2 or ITV. Not *Dallas* or *Dynasty* or even *East Enders*. No, our house in its present condition is suitable only as the site for something esoteric, sinister or perhaps merely squalid. Now Someone protested when I said we should repaint the hallway. He implied that there was nothing wrong with it as it was. He said my desire to clean it up was unreasonable and would incur unnecessary expense. I said plaintively that I wanted to put down a stair-carpet, and he said I could, so I said it was unreasonable to put down a stair-carpet in a house where the paintwork was falling off the walls. I don't know what the truth of the matter is. I only know that recourse to reason is no help at all, because we reason in different ways and arrive at diametrically opposed conclusions.

The daughter, her interest aroused by all this talk of redecoration, suggests that her own room should be painted black and hung with posters of pop stars. I can't see the reason in this because her room looks to me perfectly all right with wallpaper of lattice and roses and a white rug. She wants to sleep on the floor too, and what am I supposed to do with her brass bedstead? If this was the country I could stick it in a broken fence, but you can't do that in London. I can't see the reason behind her present mode of dress either – some friend's mini-skirt, her brother's suit jacket and somebody else's bowler hat. She has dozens of pretty frocks, but she thinks it unreasonable of me to expect her to wear them. I must take a photograph of her, because remembering the mirth occasioned by the clothes in old family albums it will be at least one thing for her grand-children to laugh at in the bleak world of the future.

I say bleak because the present is, and on the evidence so was the past. Take mouse-eating for instance. For 6000 years apparently reasonable people from Pliny through Gerard and Culpeper right down to the inhabitants of Norfolk and Suffolk in 1929 thought mice efficacious against – among other things – whooping cough and bed-wetting. To remove a deeply embedded thorn in the flesh, or to cure scorpion stings, the mouse had to be split. For internal application it had to be fried alive, then skinned. I wonder how they caught them. I wonder how on earth they persuaded anyone to eat them – although, of course, our ancestors also ingested earth worms, beetles, toads and bits of bats in the pursuit of health. Bats' blood was long believed to be a depilatory. Perhaps it is. How would we know? The Assyrians clearly didn't believe it because in the absence of Lady Grecian 2000 they used bats to turn grey hair black. Did that work? If not why did nobody say so and complain to the manufacturers? In the *Syriac Book of Medicines* we are told to dry bat's dung with lizard's dung, combine them with a number of other

Q. Have you ever _seen_ an albino bat?
A. No, er....
Q. Of course not. And you know why?
A. No, er....
Q. Because they're full of bat's blood. QED.

improbable ingredients and use the resulting mixture as eyeshadow.

I am not going to reason now but I am going to speculate, calling upon some other obscure faculty, as to the relationship between this and the modern practice of testing cosmetic preparations on the eyes of rabbits. The scientists who do this would I am sure deny accusations of barbarism and superstition, but so would Dioskorides have done had we questioned the efficacy of live mice to stop children dribbling. And so would Abd-ar-Razzaq who was making the same prescription sixteen centuries later. What I'm saying is that the much vaunted quality of reason can lead one straight up a gum tree, and I think we should drop it in favour of common sense.

PS: Pliny and Diodorus Siculus and Pomponius Mela thought mice were spontaneously generated and concluded from this that they must be life-givers. Something like that anyway. I can't *quite* follow the reasoning.

Jewels

I haven't got much jewellery. I had even less until recently. Two years ago in the country I lost a signet ring. We shook the bedclothes, upended the log baskets, raked through the ashes and crawled around on the floor like Sherlock Holmes. Nothing. Then just the other day when I was about to clear out the wood stove I discovered an old pair of rubber gloves mouldering in a corner. I usually don't bother, but since they were there I slipped them on to preserve the whiteness of the paws and was irritated to find an obstruction in the section designed to accommodate the fourth finger of the left hand. I took it to be a bit of perished rubber or a black beetle and was about to fling the gloves from me with an expression of disgust when some sixth sense prompted me to investigate further. And there was my ring. It had languished there all that long, while since the last time I had given thought to the state of the fingernails.

I used to have a lot of ear-rings. Pairs of them. I've still got quite a lot, but now they're mostly single and I can't think of anything more maddening than a single ear-ring. I don't know how the young can bear to contemplate their asymmetrical selves with one feather, cross or diamond drop. I'd almost rather have only one ear. Same with gloves – rubber, woollen or leather – one of them always gets away. And socks and stockings. I hate tights, but at least they hang together. Lose one leg, lose both. I was going to say it was strange that one never seems to lose a single shoe, but some people do. I don't know who they are or how they manage, half-shod, but frequently when we have stopped at a service station on the motorway I have observed a solitary shoe lying on the grass verges. I can only suppose that their owners have been murdered, for while the loss of one ear-ring, sock or glove does not greatly discommode a person, the loss of a shoe would cause one to hop and surely excite some remark. I can't remember ever seeing anyone going about his business with only one shoe on.

I wonder what happened to the Duchess of Windsor's shoes? Her poor husband expressed a hope that no other

woman would ever wear her jewellery, and I can't imagine
any other woman wanting to, especially that awful jewelled
bird or the ruby tassel, or the emeralds that look like a series
of boxes slung together. Tutankhamen's personal
adornments were much more tasteful and I wouldn't mind
some of them. The Orientals have always been way ahead of
us in these matters. Samia bought me a pair of little silver
ear-rings in Alexandria – following some spirited bargain-
ing – and they've been in the lobes ever since. After a
lifetime of wearing things out of Christmas crackers I
suddenly developed an allergy to base metal, and it's
farewell to what is known as costume jewellery.

But my absolutely favourite decoration of the moment is
a necklace of silver and amber beads which our beloved
Akram brought me the other day. He was out shopping in
the souks of Aleppo with his Aunt Zaffiya who was looking
for bath mitts with scratchy palms (I must remind him to tell
her to watch out for her rings when she puts them on) and
he got bored (men hate shopping) so he went off to the
silversmiths' bazaar, and as a result I am the richer.

My cousin Jeffrey called yesterday in his fire-engine –
this is another story, and I only mention it because in his
spare time he made me a pendant consisting of my name
carved in ivory and when I'm not wearing my amber beads
I'm wearing that. I'm so glad we've only got one neck. It
reduces by 50 per cent the chance of losing things. I never
used to wear my engagement ring because I was scared of
losing it, but now Providence has been so good in the matter
of the signet ring I think I'm going to chance it. After all, as
we are reminded by the Duchess of Windsor, you can't take
it with you.

No, hang on. You can. Tutankhamen did. Admittedly it
was all taken off him again, but at least it's in Cairo Museum
and no other Pharaoh will ever wear it.

Signs of spring

The country is much the same, except that some pillock has chopped down the noble Scots pines which used to grace the hill behind the house and hauled their corpses down through my 'garden'. The aforesaid garden actually consists of the top of the mountain and a field, but since Alfie planted a load of daffodils I consider myself justified in giving it this title. I have a nasty feeling that in place of the pines they are going to introduce ghastly horrible Christmas trees. These plantations are the rural equivalent of urban blight and are disfiguring altogether too much of our countryside. I wish somebody with time on his hands would start a movement to uproot the beastly things. I'd do it myself but I've been far too busy cleaning the house.

This has been one of those weeks when incidents chime together, forming coincidences. I sit in front of the telly reading a book about the son-in-law of the Prophet – and a number of Shi-ites immediately rush across the screen. I say to myself, 'I really must ring Deirdre' – and lo, the phone rings and it is she. I am hanging up the washing in the garden among the daffodils and the mud occasioned by the log-rolling operation, wondering idly why I haven't heard of any deaths since I arrived (I don't think I've ever been here for five minutes without hearing of a death) – and Janet comes back from the station announcing that she got caught up in a funeral cortege in the village.

She also brought a copy of the *Spectator* and I learn that Jeffrey's cleaning lady thinks I'm an upper-class char-woman. Well, if you leave out the upper-class part, that is precisely what I am. I've been sweeping and dusting and mopping and I even managed to tidy up a bit. Janet made me. We threw out a black bag full of single socks and halves of pyjamas and baby clothes with moth holes in. It nearly broke my heart. We threw out a number of sleeping-bag liners too. Nobody ever used them because they twine round the sleeping person constricting his movements and even his breathing. I'd left them on the floor of the cupboard, and after two years of unremitting rain they'd got damp and adhered each to the other. I *had* to throw them away, but I couldn't help thinking they'd come in frightfully handy as shrouds. I once used one as a jelly bag to strain rowan berries. If I'm not careful I shall think up further possibilities, and next thing I'll be rootling through the bin bag to get them out again.

I have thrown away a little bottle of lavender water that went rotten and smelled worse than muck-spreading, and an ancient bottle of Tabasco that lost its flavour and went pale. Perhaps because Easter is imminent, this put me into a spiritual frame of mind. The lavender water epitomises the soul of the sinner: once pure and fragrant as babies breath and now absolutely stinking. I don't know what the Tabasco signifies. Same thing I suppose – if the Tabasco lose its savour wherewith shall the Tabasco be Tabascoed? I think I'll change the name of the house to that. Tabas Coed. I always wanted a cottage called Pen-Y-Silin and I think it's true what they say about housework. It deadens the faculties and scrambles the brains. I'm not going to do it again.

When I feel stronger I must just throw away the door

mat. If I can, that is. We inadvertently left it outside and the grass is growing through it, so I shall have to wrench it away from the earth and burn it. That sounds biblical too. One minute the door mat is lying in front of the door and the next it is cast into the oven. Oh, help. Now the funeral party is leaving the graveyard and going back to the village. There's a peacock crying eerily from the hillside and I bet the ghost is plodding round the barn. I've given up the bottled sort of spirits in order to be strong and healthy and get through all the work, and this is my reward: signs and portents and scrubbing floors. I wish Jeffrey was here. Once upon a time he worked in a forest nearby. I wonder if he was planting Christmas trees or tearing them up. I do hope the latter.

PS: For some reason I can only get Irish radio here and I've just heard somebody making an impassioned plea for the planting of Christmas trees in order to create jobs.

In two minds

The third son is ill at ease and cross because people keep making him aware of superstitions that he had not previously heard of. His life used to be much simpler. He was straightforwardly annoyed the other morning when he was awakened by a bird banging on the bedroom window.

'What sort of bird?' I enquired.

'A rotten magpie,' he responded.

I went white and gasped and felt about me for somewhere to sit down. He couldn't think why I was so distressed until I explained that I could imagine no more fearful omen, and that if I'd been an Ancient Roman I should have handed in the shield and sword and pulled my toga over my head. My usual course when faced with a single magpie is to bow low and utter a Gloria; Janet affects not to recognise the creature and remarks airily, 'That was a big pied wagtit', and the son has now elected to follow the advice of Jemma and salute it with 'Good morning, Mr Magpie, how's the wife?' Since then an extremely old and distant cousin has died, but I'm not sure that that is sufficient bad luck to soak up a magpie banging on the window. Unnerved by all of this, the son put on his – no, not his, somebody else's – pullover (it's sort of grey with a chequered pattern in pink and yellow if anybody's looking for it) inside out. He was about to rectify this when everyone screamed that he mustn't, because it was unlucky. Then what was he supposed to do he enquired, half in, half out of the pullover and sounding exasperated. If he counted to nine, I told him, before changing it round, he should be all right.

Recently I read a review of a book which suggests that we all have, not one mind, but as many as a fly has facets to its eyes. The day before I read this interesting suggestion I had written in dispraise of the faculty of reason, which has never seemed to me a sufficient quality to haul us through this Vale of Tears in one piece and without getting in each other's way. I have never had much trouble simultaneously entertaining diametrically opposed propositions,

"Oh, Gawd....."

and welcome the possibility that this is not because I have one mind and am out of it, but because I have lots of them, all beavering away on their own. I know perfectly well that magpies are powerless to influence our fate or foreshadow misfortune and I also know with certainty that they jolly well can. I also know with one of my minds that another one of them knows what's going to happen tomorrow.

Apart from the above instance, I once put forward the notion that the Egyptians and the Welsh had similar tribal customs and family structures and must have common origins. One of my minds clearly took this quite seriously, or else I'd never have thought of it, would I? But the dominating mind of the time thought the whole idea frightfully funny and wildly improbable. Then, stone me, what do I read in the papers a few days later but that a respected academic has, after much research and profound concentration, come to the conclusion that the Welsh and the Berbers spring from the same stock? They've got the same genes or something. I know Berbers aren't the Egyptians, but the principle's the same, is it not? When all my minds get going at once I sometimes need reassurance.

Take this morning, for example. I was just about to wake up when I found myself complaining (silently) to an unseen person of lower rank that I had only been chosen for my present position because I was a popular and respected local man and, now that everything was over, not content with having used me they proposed to make me Area Commander, and it wasn't fair. I knew as I became aware of what one of my minds was doing that the person speaking was a native of wherever it was he was speaking from; that he was a military man, that the person he addressed was certainly inferior to him in class and rank, but that the person speaking would not have so confided in him had they not both belonged to the same military organisation. Is that clear? It may not be, because another of my minds was wondering whether there was any bread left for breakfast, whether the third son had remembered to fill the Aga, and whether I might just possibly have left a few fags in a coat pocket somewhere. As I crawled out of bed the military intruder made a final effort, indicating that he was fed up with his native heath and wanted to go for a holiday somewhere in the warm. My minds came together for a moment there.

It's freezing cold, and soon it's going to rain. And I've just seen a simply enormous pied wagtit wheeling down the valley. I think (with one of my minds) that I'll pack up and go off with the soldier.

May

Rock follies

It was quite exciting in the country. The daughter got stuck on a sheer cliff and rather took it to heart. I was carrying a pile of dirty laundry downstairs and had paused to dust a window sill with a soiled pillow case – it was going to be washed anyway – when I heard ear-splitting shrieks. She was yelling to her friends: 'Jasper, Amber, Sophie, Ja-a-a-sper ...' Dear little souls, I thought fondly – playing Red Indians or something. Then she started yelling, 'Mu-u-u-m ...' which apprised me of the fact that something was wrong. She doesn't usually expect me to join in their games. I went out of the back door and looked up at the mountain, and there she was, sitting on the rock face like a fly on fly paper. 'Come down,' I advised, and she told me at the top of her voice that she couldn't, because there was an unnegotiable drop on one side and an ants' nest on the other. She has an irrational dislike of ants. We were once lunching with some friends when our hostess asked her to nip into the kitchen and make the tea. She came back announcing to all the guests that she wasn't going to because the kitchen was full of ants – in the sink and the sugar and the butter, and running all over the table. I sensed a definite chill in the atmosphere – emanating, I believe, from our hostess.

'Come down backwards,' I howled from the safety of the

valley, and she screeched that backwards or forwards she would have to confront the ants and she wasn't going to do that either. 'Then you'll have to stay there,' I screamed, beginning to feel limp, and conscious of an awful, unmaternal mirth. Perhaps I was hysterical. Fearful lamentations, not unmixed with oaths continued to spill from the mountainside, and if she'd gone on I think she'd have alerted the Air/Sea Rescue services all by herself. Luckily Jasper appeared from the other side of the hill and led her to safety. I can't imagine how. His English teacher is related to our dear Editor and I like to think that she is in part responsible for the courage and moral fibre which he displays.

Then a friend who once chanced to be Assistant Governor of a prison came to see us and met, head on, another car in the lane to the detriment of the latter. It can have been nobody's fault because the lane curls like a corkscrew and it happens all the time, but I found that frightfully funny too. I think living in the country where you have to make your own amusements must have a curious effect on the sense of humour. I am usually much more blasé in London, but then London is seldom as thrilling.

I tell a lie. The painters are here in the London house, and I can't find anything, because it's all been moved, and this definitely eases the monotony of life. So does the obscuring layer of dust which is caused by the operation known as 'rubbing down'. It has got absolutely everywhere and none of us will be able to admit to ennui until we've washed every surface and object, and dusted every book. This should keep us entertained until the end of the century. I have sworn that this time I will truly throw away an enormous amount of things that have ceased to be useful, and keep my papers in order, and put the things that I can't bring myself to discard back in the right place. What is the right place for a broken American clock, a bowl of wax fruit (half melted) under a glass dome, two Victorian mourning frocks, a wicker-work pram, a rag doll with nail varnish all over its face? What is the right place for cats? Not really the kitchen table, or my beautiful new eiderdown, or the half-emptied suitcase in the laundry. I am beginning to think nostalgically of the barren cliff-side. The local saint lived there for years perched on a sheltered ledge, and since she was a holy person I don't suppose she had any personal effects at all. Nuns, I believe, can lay claim only to their bed and their teeth as their very own and that is why they always look so tranquil. The only pet the saint had was a hare, and hares *know* their place. You never find them dribbling on your night gown.

Nuts in May

The swarming season seems to be upon us again. It is a very bad (or good, depending on your point of view) year – for moths, that is. They must be congratulating themselves on their fecundity as they busy themselves in our wardrobes eating up our woollies. Every time I approach my clothes half a dozen moths fall out, sated. We hunted all over London for a shop which would sell us some preparation to exterminate them, before remembering that Boots would doubtless have such a product.

Our shops are so odd now we scarcely know where to go to buy anything. They seem to sell more or less everything except what you want. Boots sells sandwiches too. Janet had to tour the metropolis the other day for plain white ankle socks. All the ones in Camden Town had flowers or stripes or hearts on them, and the daughter's school doesn't permit that sort. And could we find a short-sleeved white cotton shirt? No, we couldn't. Perhaps the moths have eaten them all.

One shop has proved an unexpected bonus to the winos, who are also swarming at present. It is a very smart new shop in dark-green livery, but ill-advisedly keeps its stock of alcoholic beverages in a prominent position near the door. The older and wiser shopkeepers in Camden Town keep their stocks well behind the counter and employ a burly person to stand between the two, but this innocent new shop is learning the nature of its customers the hard way. The tedium of shopping is almost daily alleviated by lively affrays on the pavement as the manager hustles out in pursuit of fleeing winos and policemen arrive brandishing truncheons. It is interesting to note that none of the robbers say, 'It's a fair cop, guv.' They are violently aggrieved when persuaded to hand back the booty, and swear horribly as though they were the injured party.

The teenagers are swarming too. We counted eighteen of them in the garden the other day when the sun was out, and only one of them was mine. They are very young teenagers, but most of them are feet taller than any of us. The third son pointed out the strangeness of having the house overrun by enormous six-foot children. There is something Gulliverish about it. On Sunday a number of them came to lunch and while I was shoving bits of garlic in the leg of lamb and counting the potatoes because Anna and Estelle are vegetarians (I wish Cadders was: I took my eyes off the joint for a second and he ate a bit of it) there was a knock at the door and there stood a madman. He was a perfectly nice madman and no trouble really, but he wouldn't go away, and what with Cadders and the vegetarians, who have to have extra to make up for the absence of meat, there wouldn't have been enough to go round.

I collared the third son and a friend and instructed them to take the uninvited guest for a walk to the pub and lose him, but he gave them the slip and was back in no time flat. I was getting a touch unhinged myself by now because Puss had been sick under the kitchen table, and I had also been doing some tidying up, which has the effect of reducing me to tears as I find souvenirs of the dead. What with one thing and another hysteria was imminent when Someone thought of a simple device and gave him a fiver to go away. I am not usually inhospitable and once had a guest who came for a weekend, went off her head and stayed for a year, but enough is enough, is it not? It is all very well turning the mentally afflicted out 'into the community', but either the community can't cope or it can't be bothered. The poor lunatic couldn't stop talking. We had noticed him earlier sitting on a wall having a spirited conversation with himself.

In the end, overwhelmed with guilt about not sharing the lamb with the lunatic, grief about some old letters I had found, the wine I had taken for my stomach's sake and the general ghastliness of everything, I swarmed over to see Rosamond Lehmann. Anita Brookner was there too and after a while I felt better. It's a nasty old world but it can't be all bad with those two in it. Kindness and intelligence have a wonderful effect on the spirits, and Rosamond makes me think of flowers. I'm going to stop reading the newspapers and read books and think on those things that are lovely and of good report, and if anybody wants any cold lamb they can come and share it with Cadders. Sane or mad, the way I feel at present it won't make any difference.

Sugar and sex

While I was in the country I was struck by something about the nature of recantation. It was one of those secret-of-the-universe-type insights, and now I've forgotten what it was. What's more I cannot imagine what it could have been. I keep trying to remember, but all I can call to mind is those polar shifts of opinion to which the medical and scientific community are so prone, and these tend to be generational; so that when we are told the exact opposite of what we were told before it cannot be described as recantation, since it was another bloke who held the first opinion and his discipline cannot be held responsible. This, in fact, is known, not as recantation, but progress.

My two favourites concern sugar and sex. A wonderfully didactic Victorian physician was much moved by the beauty, the clear skins and bright eyes of the Turks, and since he'd never seen one without a sweetie in his mouth he concluded that sugar was the answer and directed his readers to scrape pounds of it daily off the sugar loaf and eat it all up. He seemed not to be worried by problems of obesity, spots or caries and, if he was, he doubtless attributed them to some other cause. Then there was the gynaecologist who stated categorically that the safe time for intercourse – i.e. the moment you couldn't possibly get pregnant – was precisely that moment which we are now told is the least safe. There must be many of us who led unhappy childhoods as a result of being born to surprised and aggrieved parents who had made the mistake of reading books and putting their faith in experts. Then, according to the Victorians, masturbation led inexorably to lunacy, hair loss and premature mortality, whereas nowadays the presses are inundated with DIY handbooks (Oh Lor') containing full instructions for the bashful or unenterprising, recommending the practice with apostolic fervour. 'If you don't want to lose it, use it' is the rallying cry. Of course until recently the population was encouraged to express and explore its sexuality (I think that's how they put it) on every conceivable (Oh crumbs)

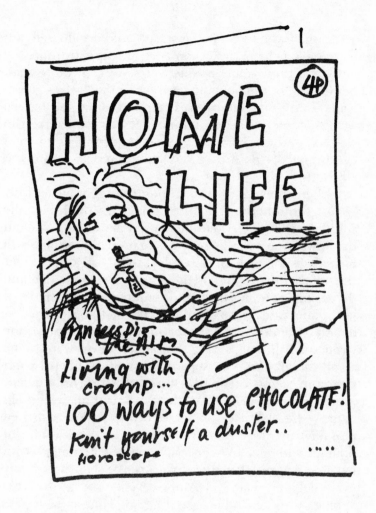

1

'The presses are inundated
with DIY handbooks...'

occasion, and now it's being sternly told it jolly well better hadn't – or *else*. AIDS, I am sure, is a great disincentive, but I also think many people will be secretly quite glad to be relieved of the necessity of hurling themselves about in Kama-Sutra-type enterprises, slipping discs and tottering wearily home in the small hours. It was rather like being stood over by a bossy physician exhorting us to eat up every one of those delicious chocolates and damn well enjoy them.

I asked Someone what he thought I might have thought about recantation, but not being a mind-reader he couldn't tell me. He told me instead about palinodes, and the unwary poet Stesichorus who gave it as his opinion that Helen was nothing more nor less than a strumpet. Today she'd have him up in the High Court in no time flat, but in those simpler times she had to content herself with striking him blind (the Victorians held that self-abuse made you blind. I wonder ... Oh never mind). At this, Stesichorus wrote his palinode, saying that Helen never went to Troy at all, at all: no, she stayed chastely in Egypt while a phantom went off and caused the furore. What a wonderful defence. Instead of 'Everything went black m'lud', she would cry, 'I never done it. I was in Egypt minding my own business and whatever went on it was a phantom doing it.' After Stesichorus had grovelled – not 'I now fully agree that there is no substance whatsoever in my allegations and I unreservedly withdraw them, apologise, etc. etc.', but 'Nay, the tale is false; never didst thou sail in the well-benched ships, never came to the towers of Troy' – he got his sight back. He was only going on what Homer had said anyway, but this is no defence in law. Libel laws have clearly always been pretty silly, and recantation only clouds the waters and makes history even more muddied and unlikely. A *phantom* – I ask you!

Gibbon wrote against the palinode. 'Where error is irretrievable, repentance is useless.' But that's his *aperçu*, not mine. Someone has put it into Latin for me: *Siquid erratum non potest revocari, sera subit paenitentia.* It would make a magnificently down beat epitaph.*

I wish I could remember why I'd started on all this. The rhododendron in the garden has recanted. Year before last it had horrible great white blowsy blooms, and I insulted it. It sulked last year, but now it has seen the error of its ways and emerged clad in small pink, much more acceptable, flowers. It's not a rhododendron any more. It's a palin-dendron.

Bottling it up

I have been compiling a little list of Things We Were Not Told. I'm not thinking about the things our leaders do not see fit to inform us of. I don't care about that at the moment. I'm thinking of things like birth and death, and how, after all the years Homo sapiens has been around, these events still take us by surprise. I didn't know childbirth was going to be like *that*, and while I always knew with every thread of my being that the death of a child was the worst that could happen I had no idea of the

---

* He also kindly put it into Greek, transliterated as follows: *ean amêchanon êi to sphalma, aporon hê metanoia.*

extraordinary dimensions, the varieties of anguish, that it could induce.

Caroline was listening to a Leading Clergyman the other day. He was offering consolation to the relations of the victims of a disaster, and he assured them that some of them might mourn for even a year. He didn't tell them that they might well go on grieving for as long as life is long. Perhaps no one had told him, and he didn't know. I've heard people rabbiting on about the stages of grief and saying that in the end we get over it. They sort of chop it up into three sections and by the time you get to the last one you're supposed to be all right. I don't know how they figured that out, but it isn't true.

The anniversary of a death came round again the other week like a cyclical tiger back to claw a bit more off one. One of the things I should be told frequently is how stupid I am. With idiot craftiness I had decided to foil Death by being away from home and refusing to acknowledge the date; with many a merry quip and a light-hearted laugh I tripped around, hither and yon, imagining I was hidden in the undergrowth and he wouldn't be able to find me. Two days later I woke up saying to Someone, 'Oh my God, I'm a conduit.' He said drowsily, 'I thought you were going to say you were a condom', and that cheered me up for a while. Nobody can say con ... anything these days without people assuming they're going to say that word.* The cheerfulness wore off. I felt exactly like a very small drain trying to contain a furious storm. I could almost hear cracking.

Beryl came round and I explained to her that I now felt like a milk bottle, vastly overfull of some corrosive that was about to overflow and flood the kitchen. So she rang a

* It's tough on the Tories

doctor, and that was a waste of time. He wanted to know
what was wrong – *you* try telling a doctor you feel like a
milk bottle. All professionals are the same – lawyers,
architects, medicos – you have to tell them what you want
them to do. I suggested hopefully to this doctor that he
might kill me, but he found that facetious and got ratty.
He wanted to hear that I had a localised pain in the third
metatarsal of the left foot or had been visited by a sudden
spasm of endogenous depression (or reactive – you pays
your money and you takes your choice) and if not
prevented was going out to put myself under a passing
truck. But one of the things I know without being told is
that suicide is a great mistake and utterly forbidden, so I
said merely that, if I could die of wanting to, I would –
now; and he said irritatedly that that was very poetic. Oh
God. Anyway it wasn't depression. I know all about
depression and this was different. This was like being a
milk bottle used for a purpose for which it was neither
designed nor sufficient. Then the quack said, very
beautifully, that he had to go and care for a sick child, so I
apologised profusely and got off the line. No wonder the
poor sods so often take to drink.

Speaking of which, in the old days when faced with the
unbearable, Beryl and I would without hesitation have
leapt straight into another sort of bottle. But I've stopped
doing that and I wouldn't let her do it either: not because
anybody told me not to, but because the time has come for
us to sit up on our rock, take a wary look round, admit how
ghastly everything is and somehow learn to put up with it.

I think I'll read some of the Prophets. They tended to a
fairly glum view of matters, and one of them – probably
Jeremiah – clearly suffered from something much worse
than endogenous depression. He was way off his head. I'm
not going to take much heed of what they have to tell me –

none of them ever said he felt like a milk bottle, so I can't relate to them – but when I'm really low I don't want to read P.G. Wodehouse. When I'm really, really low only Strindberg makes me laugh. *The Father* once had me rolling round in hysterics. Maybe I'm incorrigible and people have been trying to tell me things for ages. Perhaps it's just that I haven't been listening.

'she's feeling low...'

June

Front-line bulletin

I may have said this before and if I haven't it is probable that somebody else has, so if you think you're going to be bored just skip this next bit.

Always remember, *mes enfants, mes amis,* that things are never so indescribably ghastly that they can't get worse. This is not a consoling thought, but it does lend to life a certain grim interest. What next, you ask yourself as you lie on your back where fate has flung you amidst the sweet violets. People have sometimes asked, eyeing me quizzically, whether I don't perhaps exaggerate, embroider a trifle in these communiqués from the Home front. 'Well no, sugar,' I respond, after a moment's reflection. 'No, I don't exaggerate.' Sometimes I go on to mutter, 'You don't know the *half* of it.' Take last week, for example. I'm not going to tell you about one particular day which is etched for ever on my mind, because first it would be unfair to what seemed like quite a large proportion of the population who for one reason or another kept pouring in through the garden gate, and second, you wouldn't believe it. You can ask Beryl if you like. She had to lie down again. At one point the third son stood on the balcony going 'Act 4, scene 3, take 14.' If you can imagine a collaboration between Ibsen and Brian Rix you'll have something of the flavour, and I wasn't feeling too strong already. The annoying thing was that we had a camera crew to hand, only they were up in the Buildings photographing Someone for a TV programme. I'm sure it will be very good [it was], but it won't have the *je ne sais quoi* of the matchless performances that were going on down here. The Labour party canvasser made a brief guest appearance and, as somebody remarked, all that was lacking was the Avon Lady. The Avon Bard might have picked up a few pointers too.

I'm watching telly at the moment. Vincent van Gogh has just painted his *Sunflowers* and Gauguin says he doesn't want to be loved. I don't think he need worry, he doesn't seem very nice. Now he's trying to paint a picture in a high wind and getting into a fearful rage. Nevertheless their lives appear tame compared to my own, so I'm turning them off. I don't want to watch any ear-lopping either. Vincent did say he had something simmering in a pot and I wondered.

I also wonder what Jeffrey will make of Egypt and what compulsion it is that drives the denizens of the back columns of the *Spectator* to visit this ancient and mysterious land. (Oh lawks. I just turned the telly on again and Vincent's done it. He's all bandaged up.) As I was saying, I wonder if Jeffrey's going to enjoy sculling down the Nile. (Poor old Vincent's gone right round the twist. He's roaring. His doctor says he suffers from symptoms of extreme terror. Don't we all?) Back to the Nile. When I went on it I got bitten by a lot of beastly namoosas, which is what we Arabic scholars call the common mosquito, and I hope Jeffrey has made special arrangements because unless he has he will find that his ice cubes are cooling nothing more than a glass of 7-Up. Egypt is becoming increasingly Islamic and alcohol is hard to come by if you don't know the right people. It also has other spectacular

forms of insect life besides namoosas: flying beetles almost as big as little cats, and things that live in the sewers until they come up for a stroll round: nasty things. However, I didn't notice any slugs, so Jeff won't need to worry about that. I was told there were snakes in the fields but I didn't see any of them either.

In fact I found Egypt quite peaceful after Camden Town – except for the traffic which beggars description – and I rather wish I was there now. Vincent's gone and there's nothing on telly except for Tom and Jerry, which is too violent for me, cricket, another silly game, and a lady talking about the election. Any minute it'll be *Songs of Praise* and I shall have no choice but to go and read the newspapers. Instead of being thankful for this period of Sunday boredom, I find myself at a loss. I believe actors feel the same way when they're off stage, and I must

78

remember to watch Lawrence Olivier tonight 'revealing some secrets about his professional technique'. I may gather a few tips. I wouldn't wish to return to the histrionics of the past week, but it isn't half dull when the curtain comes down.

PS: The fifth son has just arrived in black-face, clad from head to toe in Combat Gear. Things are looking up again. Or do I mean down again? Exit, pursued by a bear.

Millionaire's row

I nearly got thrown out of Christies last week. I went with Caroline, and I *had* been asked, only I hadn't got a ticket. It was a glittering auction in benefit of an AIDS charity, but they were loth to let us in. Rain was threatening, photographers were lined up both sides of the door, there were policemen in the road and some elegant ladies on the steps when we arrived – and the doors were firmly closed. Why was this, we all asked each other, but no one knew. A multi-millionaire arrived in a chauffeur-driven limousine, strode up the steps and rang the bell.

The door opened a crack and a man asked what he wanted.

'To bid,' responded the millionaire.

Slam went the door.

Several more millionaires got the same treatment, and

so did Caroline and I who had been instructed to arrive at 6. The man behind the *slam* kept asking people if they had come to help. It seemed that an intention to bid was not due and sufficient cause to get in out of the rain. The doors opened and we all surged forward again, but they had opened only to let a man and some dogs out. I've never watched a number of irate millionaires before. They looked much like anyone else in a rage, only better-groomed.

When everyone was finally admitted the staff baulked at me. They utterly refused to consider letting me in without a ticket and were just about to hurl me out when the lady who had organised the whole thing came into view and said it was OK. The staff looked disappointed. We were then hustled and bustled and ticked off by a series of people in uniform. Caroline reached for a glass of champagne and was told to make haste. You can't really make haste taking a glass of champagne. It's one of those things that everyone does at the same rate, unless, of course, smitten with the palsy. If you do it in an unseemly rush you spill it.

'Move along there,' ordered another flunkey.

We ended up cowering in a back room, and after looking furtively round for officials I lit a ciggie. Caroline said I was brave, not to say reckless, and sure enough yet another person in uniform appeared as if by magic and took it off me. I sulked in a corner until Boy George stalked in and promptly lit up. Right, I thought, if he can I can, and before you could say emphysema practically everyone in the place was puffing away like mad. No ashtrays, naturally, as smoking was forbidden, so out of consideration for the parquet and odd bits of boule-and-marquetry that stood around we dropped the stubs in other people's glasses of champagne.

It was diverting to see what everyone had thought it appropriate to wear for this evening. Dress ranged from black velvet and pearls (Boy George) to a sports jacket, orange mini-skirt, lisle stockings and gym shoes (a lady I believe to be a pop star). I didn't see Fergie because I was riveted to the spot by the necessity of remaining adjacent to the glass of champagne I was putting dog ends in. I really must give up smoking. But I did see a lady from East Enders and Shirley Bassey. I met a neighbour from the country too and we wailed about the weather conditions which invariably deteriorate as you approach Llanrheaedr-ym-Mochnant. I had feared we might be bored at an auction, but we weren't a bit. Everyone was talking at the top of their voices while the bidding went on. After a while my legs began to give way and there were no chairs in the room where we were. Then I noticed a baize-covered table empty of lots. There was a duchess perched on one end, and next to her the godfather of the eldest son. Encouraged by this happy circumstance, I sat on the table, only somebody had emptied a glass of champagne on it – probably to free the glass for further dog ends – and I sat in that. I was also clad in black velvet which doesn't readily dry, and I can't summon words to describe the disagreeableness of wearing champagne-soaked velvet next to the skin. The evening was reaching a crescendo. The auctioneer suddenly howled into his microphone, 'Will you all *shut up*.' Caroline and I agreed it was time to go home. Despite the faintly less-than-welcoming ambience, I believe the auction raised a larger sum for charity than ever before. This is due to the magnificent efforts of the lady who organised the whole thing. Praise heaven she was there to prevent me being bounced. I wouldn't have missed it for anything.

Waterlogged

The bread bin was full of rain the other morning, and half loaves were floating in it like fish. There is a leak in the roof of the back kitchen, and sometimes rain runs down the electrical wiring and makes everything go bang and then out. One day we'll have it mended. It's made of tar, and there's no way of getting to it directly from the road, so the menders will have to plod through the house with buckets of molten, peculiar-smelling black stuff, and I am rather putting off the moment. Presumably they won't be able to do anything while it's actually raining anyway, and as it always is we may have water-logged bread for some time. We have all been trying not to go on and on about the weather, since it is so pointless, but when the sky darkens to deepest black-green at 4 o'clock in the afternoon it is difficult not to pass some remark. Cheated of toast on that rainy morning, I warmed up some rolls from the freezer and we breakfasted on rolls and honey to the sound of thunder. I am sure I've never done that before, as thunder is seldom around so early. It usually creeps up on the afternoons, or more spectacularly roars in the night time.

Dispirited by the soggy conditions prevailing at home we splashed our way to a restaurant for lunch. There were little jars of cornflowers on each table and also four unused wax crayons in primary colours. 'Why,' asked Someone of the waitress, 'are there wax crayons on the table?'

'So you can draw on the tablecloff,' said the waitress, surprised at our obtuseness. Of course. I have been known to draw on the tablecloth, but faced with this blatant encouragement I could think of nothing to portray. Instead I gazed out of the window at a man in dark glasses smoking marijuana and drinking ale from a can. After a while along came another man with a sack. He stopped by the first man, dipped into his bag and brought out an empty beer can. This he offered in exchange for man A's full can. When man A, not unreasonably, refused, man B dipped again into his bag and came up with an empty and *squashed* beer can. When this too was rejected, he ambled amiably off. Luckily for me the third son had also been watching this scene or I should have doubted the evidence of my senses.

Somehow the third son has recently often been a fellow-witness to curious happenings. 'If you don't believe me you can ask *him*,' I say, pointing. I was able to help him through one episode. We were visiting my Mama in hospital when a poor woman was wheeled in from the operating theatre. She looked not at all well, being the approximate colour of our thundery afternoons and barely conscious. The son, sitting with his back to her, suddenly heard a nurse say, 'Would you like your husband to come and take a photo of you before you die?' I know that's what he heard because that was the way I heard it too. An expression of absolute incredulity established itself on the son's face, but I was able to reassure him. I had glanced sharply up at these remarkable words and since I was facing the patient and nurse I did not have to rely solely on my hearing. I had seen the nurse indicating a large and elaborate floral tribute and it was this that she was suggesting should be recorded for posterity.

We all had our photos taken at Rex's birthday party yesterday. He and Zé did a beautiful be-bop dance to Glen Miller music and everyone yelled at him to pick her up. So he did, only he dropped her. I was pleased to see another hostess lying on the floor giggling uncontrollably. I talked for a long time to a completely fascinating man whose name I had not caught. He was widely travelled, had met almost everyone, and was not only erudite but amusing.

I said to Zé, 'That was a most interesting person. Who is he?'

'That's Dickens, you fool,' she snapped.

It wasn't, of course. It was another famous author.

In the end I did talk about the weather to some other people. One girl held it was the result of underground atomic explosions pushing the earth's plates apart, but the only military man present said it was the result of underarm deodorants in aerosol cans messing up the ozone layer. *Chacun à son gout.*

Mad talk

When I've got a minute I'm going to write a book called *Osmosis and Institution* or maybe *Institution and Osmosis*. Not merely because I greatly fancy this as a title, but because I am beginning to wonder about the precise

84

nature of the membranous walls which separate those of us who are inside from those of us who are outside. Take universities, for instance. I know some idiots who reside in universities and some very smart people who help me out round the house. The criminal population is unfairly distributed, with many villains holding respectable positions and a number of innocents incarcerated. I know doctors who I would not have thought could have got a CSE in breathing, while I met a madman living in the streets of Alexandria who spoke four languages fluently and expressed himself in all of them with grace and what, in the sane, would have been described as intelligence; and what has given rise to this reflection is my recent visit to a lunatic asylum.

I don't suppose they're called this any more. I expect they're called Temporary Shelters for the Rather Upset, or something, but that's what they're supposed to be: asylums for the mad. Patrice, who has a friend in one of them, injudiciously used this term to one of the charge nurses and was reproved. 'We do not call people mad in here,' he said. 'Well, what do you call them?' asked Patrice. 'We say they have a little breakdown,' he said.

Sometimes this description is far from adequate. There are people in there (and out here) who need to be kept under lock and key: some because they are a danger to themselves, and some because they are a danger to others. They are 'sectioned' for a while. (This is what we now say, rather than 'certified', and I don't see why it should be considered euphemistic. It will soon, if it does not already, carry exactly the same connotations.) But there seem to be very few curbs on their movements, and it also is very difficult to pin down a person in authority who will give a measured opinion or prognosis of any particular case. I sympathise to a certain extent. Madness is not only confusing to everyone involved, but infectious.

None the less professionals who choose to earn their money in this field do seem to be uniquely elusive when questions are being asked. Patrice has been castigated for not telephoning for information (uncaring) and for telephoning (hassling). She is beginning to feel a little crazy herself. The top doctor wears a red carnation in his buttonhole and she finds this odd. It could be construed as eccentric to consider a carnation-wearer potty. On the other hand, when you come to think of it, a person with a carnation who is not going to a wedding could well be seen as rather strange, especially in the NHS. It somehow does not relate to the real world.

I went with Patrice to see her friend and, going up the stairs, was clapped on the back by a person in dark glasses who said, 'Darling, wonderful to see you again.' I had never seen him before in my life, but then this happens at parties all the time. A drunk turned up in our house the other evening and imagined himself to be in an Italian restaurant, and me the proprietor. We had a really barmy conversation until I tottered to bed wondering about the parameters of sanity. Someone got him out of the house at 5 o'clock the next morning. I can't think how he got himself home, but I would have done anything to get rid of him and I didn't care where he was going. This reminded me of the asylum, where the doors and gates are all unlocked, and I wondered whether the authorities felt the same as me. Do they think to themselves on an 'unconscious level', as we analysts put it, that their charges might as well go and take their 'chances in the community'? Are they just utterly fed up with the whole thing? The mad, being obsessed, generate great energy and feeling. The ostensibly sane, being, on the face of it, concerned only with getting home the groceries, can find themselves overwhelmed.

Patrice's friend said to her as we left, 'You'd better get me out of here, otherwise I'm going to go insane.'

As we walked to the bus a bird flew past. Her friend is frightened of birds, thinking them to be aliens.

'They do look a bit dodgy,' said Patrice thoughtfully. 'Maybe ...'

Yes, well – maybe.

July

Getting warmer

I can't help it. I'm going to talk about the weather. I can't
think of anything else. It seems that Greece has got the sun
– all of it – and foreign visitors were recently advised to
stay indoors rather than inspect the Acropolis or go and
watch the natives beating squids to death on the rocks by
the seaside. New York, too, I am told was rather warm.
Janet has somehow deduced that if we took ourselves
somewhere in Middle Europe we would just about get it
right. I don't know what her reasoning is, and anyway it's
an impractical idea because we've got to stay here. The
school hols haven't started yet. This is incredible since I
keep thinking it must be autumn. I don't know why I think
this, seeing as we've had no summer – but that is my
impression. Rather than hoping for better weather in what
remains of this year, I have despaired and am waiting only
for the frosts of winter. Every now and then Janet puts on
a summer frock, but she is whistling in the dark. Very
dark. Caroline rings to say that she can't see to write even
in the daytime, and I go to sleep each afternoon as the
drawing-room grows crepuscular with the daily, encroach-
ing storm.

Gwynne brought a terrible cold back from Russia (I
forgot to ask what the weather was like there) and passed it
on to some of us. One of us took it to the Lake District

Aaaaaa-chi...chorrya!!

where Jemma is playing in *Miss Julie* and I couldn't decide whether it would or would not enhance the quality of her performance in this particular drama. Janet has sore eyes and we are puzzled as this is usually caused by hay fever and I cannot imagine that pollen is getting around very much. Surely it must all be lying in the gutters in the form of soup, mixed up with the rain. The daughter too has just come home from school with a temperature and a white face, and maybe the Middle Europe idea isn't such a bad one after all. Then, on the other hand, there are Gwynne's dreadful Soviet sneezes. Perhaps nowhere is safe between the rain and the pollen. Perhaps we are doomed to spend the rest of our lives indoors. I did hope for a while that as it was raining at Wimbledon the telly might show some old films instead, but it didn't. It showed old tennis.

The third son took the plunge and decided to travel to the South of France to see what the weather was doing there. His passport had run out, so he went to the Post Office for a form. The Post Office had run out of forms. They suggested he ring around to see if he could find a Post Office which had a supply of these rare documents. None of them had. They said perhaps he should try the suburbs. In the rain? It seems they were on strike at Petty France, so at least he couldn't get wet queuing down there.

The eldest son stayed dry doing jury service, but that too sounds a dispiriting experience. A number of people seemed to have been arraigned (there goes the weather again) more on misfortune than misdemeanour, and most of them were found not to be guilty. Human nature being what it is, we had rather hoped for something spectacular in the way of crime and were faintly disappointed. They were all let out into the streets and the downpours, but I suppose it's preferable to being held on remand. Mary also was on jury service recently and found the criminals less alarming than some of the jurors, one of whom embraced embalming as a hobby and liked nothing better than to regale anyone who would listen with the details of this unusual skill.

I must forget about the weather and get on with *Osmosis and Institution*, or should it be *Institution and Osmosis*. I am warming to the theme of who belongs in and who out. A figure in authority was absent from court on the first day of Royal Ascot and we have drawn our own conclusions. What would he have said if the prisoner had failed to turn up because he preferred to be at the races? I hope it was raining.

Tripping up

I had a medical check-up a while ago and, if I am to believe the man in charge, the entire staff of the laboratory where they do these things was laid low by the fumes emanating from a phial containing a fluid ounce or two of the substance that runs (or perhaps 'lurches' is the *mot juste*) through my veins. He went on so long and eloquently that I have been shamed into total abstinence.

I did try to explain feebly that my blood was Russo-Finnish and all the Russo-Finns had blood like that, but the man (who I think is a Muslim) pooh-poohed this excuse and said he'd never seen anything like it. Stung, I removed myself from the occasions of sin – London parties, the pan cupboard in the back kitchen where I conceal the Scotch – and went for a solitary ride on the wagon. The maddening thing is that when I am alone I don't miss alcohol in the least – not a twinge, not a tremor, not a craving – but when it's there and other people are knocking it back I find it irresistible. Beryl is like me when it comes to abstaining in company. I say to her, 'Have a drink, lamb-chop', and she says, 'Certainly-not-oh-alright-thank-you-very-much', all in one breath. We are deficient in moral fibre. I'm afraid. One of the parties I missed was the *Spectator*'s, and another was my own. I do hope everyone had a good time.

Now we come to life's little ironies. I have never fallen over while drunk, or if I have I don't remember. Awash with clear mountain water (except I think it's got naturally occurring lead, radio-activity and dead sheep in it), I fell on my face. Wearing a galabeya for comfort and coolness, and carrying a tray, I tripped upstairs. Had I had the drink taken this would not have happened. For one thing, I wouldn't have wanted any supper and therefore wouldn't have been carrying a tray, and for another when I'm on automatic I'm much, much more careful. Everyone who is accustomed to wearing long skirts when three sheets to the wind knows perfectly well that in order to ascend steps with any hope of achieving the summit you need to hoick them up between finger and thumb so that the hem clears your feet, and tread carefully. Normally I do this when I've had a glass of sherry, but this time, sanguine with sobriety, I didn't. And I didn't drop the tray in order to save myself either – because the insouciance in relation to a bit of china and a wodge of bread and cheese which a tot of Bristol Cream induces in one was absent in me. I'm going to have to adjust all my reactions.

The unexpectedness, and the unfairness, of this turn of events reminds me for some reason of one of the sayings of Janet. She says that women's magazines always advise in their cookery columns that if you wish to give a dinner in order to impress somebody (usually a man, if you haven't got him yet, and his boss if you have) you must offer a dish with which you are entirely familiar and which you have prepared many times before. This, says Janet, is a load of old cobblers. Over-confident, careless and bored stiff with your speciality, you will burn it, or curdle it, or forget to put it in the oven. What you should do is look up in a cookery book some intensely elaborate Indonesian or Mongolian dish full of ingredients you have never even

'What you should do is look up
in a cookery book some intensely
elaborate Indonesian or Mongolian
dish...'

heard of, and this will keep you on your toes. The ultimate subtlety is then to pretend, when it lies steaming on the table, that you frequently throw it together when you feel like relaxing from the more demanding aspects of the home cuisine.

She's quite right of course. She usually is, and when I've completed *Osmosis and Institution* – or *should* it be *Institution and Osmosis*? – I shall compile an anthology of her utterances so that everyone can have the benefit. The only trouble is that what I didn't say earlier – not wanting to boast – is that I've given up smoking too, and I find it very, very difficult to write – or do anything – without a fag clenched between the teeth. I may never do anything ever again.

The test will come when I return home in a day or two. 'If I cannot drink my sherry when all around are slurping theirs, nor beg a fag from a passing teenager …'

It's going to be awfully difficult. Oh, well. I never wanted to be a man anyway.

Umbrella cover

I believe I am responsible for the recent pleasant weather. A couple of weeks ago when it was still relentlessly raining I penned a few words on the subject, and before they went to press the fine spell was upon us. Human nature being what it is, once the sun came out everybody forgot what it was like when it was raining, so my words appeared dated, meaningless and perverse. I wish I'd thought of doing it earlier. We could have had a longer summer. It's not as though I didn't know what would happen. It's the same sort of thing as carrying an umbrella before the day has decided what type of day it should be, which is not so much insurance as a kind of primitive magic. Before the rain stopped we were driving down Harley Street on our way to John Lewis in the pursuit of hooks-and-eyes and passed Janet's favourite inscription announcing that Florence Nightingale left her hospital on this site when she went off to the Crimea. Janet observed that it was jolly considerate of her, because otherwise the people we saw ascending the steps would have been sitting in the pissing rain as they waited to consult a medical person.

The third son has been in the hands of medical personnel in France. The good news is that he is still alive, and the bad news is five cracked ribs. It seems that the car in which he was being driven turned over three times (bad news) but that a party of off-duty ambulance men was passing at the time (good news). The awful thing about having a lot of children is that one has so many lives to lose. Even your own takes on added importance as you reflect that should you get reaped they will never be able to find their clean socks or remember to carry an umbrella. I wish I could shake myself free of blind superstition. It was the third son upon whose window a magpie tapped earlier in the year. I hold magpies in fearful respect; bowing to solitary ones and uttering incantations and prayers. I know the wretched creature was either engaged in combat with its own reflection, or trying to eat the putty which holds some hidden attraction for all the birds of the valley, but am not reassured.

After the euphoria induced by the news that the boy still

lived I began to flap about internal injuries and wonder what the Frogs call lungs and spleen. The eldest son reminded me acidly that his brother was the guest, not of some twit, but of darling Professor Sir Alfred Ayer, who is the cleverest man in Europe if not the world, and if he said all was well then I could surely take his word for it. I know, I know, but what a wonderful target for free-floating anxiety is an accident to a loved one in a foreign country. When the dishwasher contrived to expel water from some unsuspected orifice all over the adjacent china shelves I took it very coolly, merely standing ankle deep in suds and wondering whether ribs heal straight, now that it is no longer medical policy to bind them up or encase them in plaster. I am sunk in depression at this gratuitous reminder of the frailty of flesh and bone. I have also just finished a novel – writing one, not reading one. I can read two in a day with no trouble at all, but writing the things takes time and thought, and now that Someone has sent it off to the printer I feel like a dog whose bone has been stolen. I can't think quite what I'm for, except to function as a machine for worrying, and that is really no fun.

Oh, well, the school holidays have begun, so it's back to the country next week and the magpies. The only good thing is that I seem to remember that as the summer draws on they get more sociable, cease going around on their own, and flock in fields in great numbers leaving silver and gold and a secret never to be told well behind. And if I take an umbrella, even the rain may hold off. Some skunk has pinched my raincoat, and if whoever it is is superstitious I give him warning that if ever I discover his identity I shall put his name in a drawer.

Pushing the boat out

I did it again. I went on about the weather and it changed. The bread-bin got waterlogged, and many people found themselves unable to play bowls. I was, myself, quite pleased about that as the TV showed a film instead, but it must have been sickening for the would-be contestants and, I suppose, for the two or three devotees who actually like watching this game being played. A lady has written to me suggesting that I move the bread-bin out of the drips, so I have. I have put it on the New World gas cooker, which stands by in case the weather should ever get too hot to keep the Aga running.

Today began in a very startling fashion with torrential rain, an indignant blackbird warning off would-be intruders on his territory by going chick, chick, chick for what seemed like hours in the irritating way that blackbirds have; and then the burglar alarm of one of the neighbours went off. It is interesting that when this happens it absolutely never occurs to one that it could mean that burglars are actually attempting an ingress. Everybody invariably assumes that the cat has tripped the wire, or the householder has forgotten to throw some switch, and they get annoyed as the racket goes on and on. If I were a burglar I shouldn't be in the least alarmed, knowing that the people around would be muttering and cursing, with their fingers in their ears, rather than flying to the phone to dial 999, or approaching with the poker and a challenging question.

All this was happening at about 5 am, and shortly afterwards an unpleasant wind got up. When I eventually got up myself Someone handed me the post, which was remarkable only in that it consisted of a brochure from a company which hires out – or rather charters – yachts to the public – at some expense. We have no idea how it occurred to these people to contact us or even how they knew we existed, but they clearly have an unrealistic idea of our means. These vessels are not DIY but come complete with crew, captains most usually being described as skilled, excellent, and British. Frequently the remaining crew are expert, multi-lingual and European. One of the captains is gracious too (I can't quite picture a gracious captain. How does he manifest this quality at sea in a Force 11?). Some of the captains are American, skilled and personable, one is Australian and expert, and one, rather daringly, is French. He and the cook are both categorised as enchanting: another quality I should not put at the head of a list of those desired in a sea captain (or even a sea cook). How does he measure up on keeping the thing afloat is what I would want to know? It's all entirely academic anyway since the tariff puts all these skilled British and European sailors well beyond our reach. I'm rather sorry, because it would be nice to sail away from the rain sitting on a wide deck which 'sports cushions and mattresses for sun-bathing and a teak table on the foredeck for *al fresco* meals'. Some of them have air-conditioning, ice-makers, water-makers, comprehensive navigational and powerful communications equipment, and I rather like the order of importance in which they are listed. It is perversely reassuring that the compilers of the brochure should place comfort before safety, as though the latter could be taken for granted. I was recently invited to go sailing in a much smaller vessel off the south coast but declined since, no matter how excellent etc. are our British captains, our British waters leave something to be desired compared with the Mediterranean. If I'm going to get wet I prefer to do it on dry land.

When our ship comes in we will push the boat out and avail ourselves of the 'endearing motor sailer' with its rich carpeting and polished brass fittings and green plants. Or the one with 'the bleached teak decks' with their 'exceptional lounging space and unusually large cushioned circular cockpit'. Or perhaps we'll settle for the experienced British captain and his gourmet chef and

'If I'm going to get wet, I prefer
to do it on dry land'

skilled deck crew. Or maybe we'll go on the cruise offered in yet another brochure (why are we showered with these tantalising documents?). British officers again and a barman, nationality unspecified, who will mix us an ice-cold pina colada. No – hang on – we won't. There's a comedian on this boat who 'has you rolling in the aisles'. I don't like the sound of that. He's bound to be British and probably Northern. I shall stay at home and watch the bread sailing in the bread-bin.

August

The stuff of myth

I have just resurrected a piece of embroidery – well, appli-
qué mostly – which I began about twenty years ago and got
fed up with. It represents Persephone and Pluto – only I
prefer to call him Dis, because otherwise I have this vision of
big floppy ears – and is crammed with mythical characters
made out of bits of felt and silk and velvet and rep.

Now I've forgotten who most of them are. The
distraught appearing piece of pink cotton in the middle
distance must, I think, be Demeter searching for her
daughter (God, I do know the feeling: the school hols find
me constantly on the phone tracking my one down, or, in
the country, scouring the hills and hollows screeching her
name), but I haven't yet given her a head or hands. The
three ladies in black on the right are almost certainly the
Furies because one of them has got hair made of bootlaces
(snakes: did the Furies have adders for hair?). There's a
harpy poised above the throne and I can't remember why
she's there. Are there harpies in Hades, or has she dropped
in out of some other myth? And who are the three ladies
on the left wearing white and so far all bald? The Graces?
Were they around in this story? I obviously chickened out
of putting Cerberus in my picture. According to some
versions he had three heads, but according to others he
had a hundred. Even three is too many for me, and
anyway I don't think I've left room for him. There are

three streams of Lethe emerging from under the throne, which suddenly, for the first time, caused me to see this piece of Attic furniture as a commode, and reflect that the attic would be the best place for it. These streams are composed of snippets from an old grey watered taffeta ballgown and would be quite easy to unpick, so if I pulled myself together I could replace them with a horrendous three-headed dog. Maybe I could make him out of fake fur, or would he look too poodly? I see Cerberus really as one of those sleek-coated, short-tempered hounds who bare their teeth and tear you limb from limb before you can say 'Good boy'. Velvet, I think. Black. Where am I going to find a bit of black velvet without cutting up my best coat and skirt?

I wondered for some time why I'd put the Graces (good) on the left (sinister) side and the Furies (bad) on the right. Then I remembered that the sinister is the distaff side, and that this is really the story of Demeter and Persephone, and decided that twenty years ago I must have sat down and worked it out and tacked down all my bits of cloth accordingly. I shall have to reread the tale and discover whether my cast is entitled to be present, or whether the younger me had Cecil B. de Mille qualities and an inability to see why she shouldn't put Moses in the Wars of the Roses.

There's a nice little Doric temple made of white satin, but I'm not altogether satisfied with the clouds of pale grey tweed. I think I may replace them with a slice of foam from a shoulder pad. I have got less purist with the course of time. If I do start doing all this fine stitching again I shall have to cut my fingernails, because my fingers are tripping over them. I could paint the clippings white and use them for Cerberus's teeth. I have got to go through the wardrobe too and throw out millions of moth-eaten garments. First, I shall have to consult Someone about the ins and outs of the legend, and then I'll have to ask if I can have most of his old ties to cut up and create fields of asphodel, because I think some of them have got flowers on. I wish it was pomegranates. As it is, I shall have to embroider one with silks, which is difficult. Or perhaps I could paint a button. I'll probably lose the sight of my eyes with all this fiddly work, but it would be satisfying to finish it. Twenty years is a long time to leave unfinished business.

Sleeping sickness

This is going to be awfully boring. You know what mothers say – only boring people are ever bored. Don't believe it. I'm sure you're not yourself intrinsically boring, and nor, I like to believe, are Janet and I, except at present. We are bored to bits, and it is this that has rendered us boring. We are suffering lethargy to the point of narcolepsy; going to bed at eight, waking up at ten and falling asleep in the afternoon. This is due to the deeply horrible nature of the month of August and the fact that the drain is blocked again. Janet washed all the towels and hung them on the line and they got more or less dry, and then it rained and they got wet again. They're still on the line, and we can't wash anything else until the drain gets unblocked, so they might as well stay there. The daughter and Lucy and Amber and Jessie, Lucy's dog, went swimming in the stream, and the girls, who for some reason swim in their wellies, got them full of water and soaked their jeans. Listlessly I hung them over the Aga, and they got scorched. (The jeans, that is.) So far the girls haven't noticed, but when they do I expect they'll be furious, which is curious (I always think a rhyme makes things less boring), since they put a lot of time and effort into tearing huge holes in their trousers in order to be fashionable. Perhaps *their* boredom will be alleviated for a moment or two by rage. I can't even be bothered to be cross. Jessie shook herself dry in the sitting-room and I only opened one eye like a crocodile and then closed it again.

It all began a few days ago as we drove down to the country. The motorway was as blocked as the drain, so we took the A road and that was blocked too. We turned on the radio in the hope of some diversion and got the news. The news is boring in August, and spy stories are always boring, fiction or fact, since it seems impossible to arrive at the truth. Politicians also find trouble in dealing with this commodity, handling it like a housemaid with greasy fingers. We were briefly galvanised by an item about low-flying aircraft, because they frequently brutally break into our trance here in the country. Somebody on the pro-gramme suggested they should do their manoeuvres in Turkey or Labrador and Janet and I agreed that that would be all right, since then they'd only madden the odd Anato-lian peasant or a few retrievers. Jessie, who's a labrador-retriever, is already kept on the *qui vive* by our own low-flying aircraft. We ground our teeth for a while as we thought of the cost to the tax-payer of these pointless flights, and then we listened to the *Archers*, which is usually quite rewarding. But it was all about Mr Grundy picking flowers and Mrs Snell objecting and somebody else laugh-ing his head off. We couldn't follow it at all. Then there was a lady cooking something on *Woman's Hour* and I don't think you can cook on the wireless. It doesn't really work.

Then there was something described as a 'play', only it didn't seem to be. It seemed to be one chap doing a monologue, and it was so madly boring Janet went to sleep while she was driving. She had to eat a lot of strong mints to keep awake, and I had to rack my brains to think of interesting things to tell her to keep her alert. At the sight of the first conifer plantation I told her again about the wonderful scheme whereby the government makes rich people richer by giving them subsidies or tax relief to plant these obnoxious trees and ruin the countryside. She knew about it already, of course, but the reminder stirred her adrenalin and we reached our destination in one piece. There are new conifer plantations all over the moors, so when we find ourselves getting too catatonic I suppose all we need do is go out and contemplate them. We haven't got the energy to get into a real temper, but irritation will doubtless keep us from lapsing into total slumber.

Off balance

Why don't I shut up. I should never have moaned that August was boring. As soon as I said that, Janet's cat, Eric, lost his tail. We don't know how. He can't say, and speculation is fruitless. He lives near the railway lines, but his tail was not initially utterly severed, only almost. The vet had to amputate it. Eric has made a good recovery but lost his balance. He went out to sit on the wall in the sun, and when he saw Janet he made to leap off and greet her in his accustomed, graceful feline fashion, but that didn't

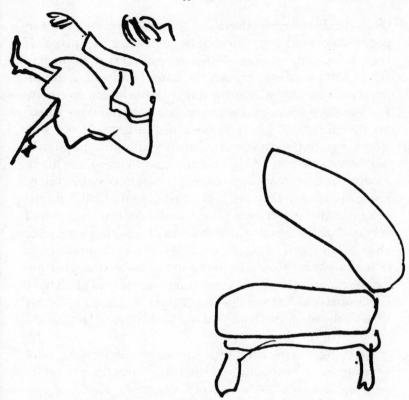

work. He fell off. Janet had to stifle a laugh and now her guilt is insupportable.

Then the daughter got glandular fever. Most of our sons have had this unpleasant and debilitating illness, but only as O or A Levels approached. The daughter is not yet threatened by these events and I don't know why she should be struck down in the middle of the summer hols. Her throat swelled prodigiously as we sat alone in remote seclusion at the end of the valley. When she couldn't even swallow saliva I telephoned for medical assistance and now we're in the children's ward of the local hospital with cut-out teddy bears on the doors and a rabbit on the window pane. I kept telling her she'd be better soon, and putting off the phone call, so when I sent for the doctor night had fallen and we sailed through the lanes in an ambulance in the dark. I had an interesting talk with the ambulance man, and the doctor was a great fan of Jeffrey's; the nurses here are delightful and I have a friend in another mummy with whom I go to the canteen for lunch (chips and shepherd's pie, or quiche and chips, or chips), so I can't claim to be lonely, but I am amazingly cut off. One telephone is full of money so cannot be used, and when I tried another one to call London I could hear Janet but she couldn't hear me. I reversed the charges then, because I was sick of giving British Telecom ten pences for nothing, like throwing buns to a bear who refuses to perform. I feel as though I am living in a grounded space-ship, and very soon I shall have nothing to read but women's magazines, because I've nearly read all the old paperbacks I slung hastily into an overnight bag as we left.

Speaking of overnight, I spent my first night here sleeping in a mechanical armchair which extended to permit one to recline but also sprang back to position at a fingertip's touch, nearly catapulting the occupant across the room. Last night I got to sleep in the camp-bed because the mummy who had slept in it the night before had been moved into a room. It's all a bit complicated. It's the nurses I feel sorry for. At the moment the place isn't too crowded, but they have the wary look of people who are used to being overwhelmed and have got in the way of expecting it. One day there were only two of them on duty with nine ailing children to mind. Sister was juggling a baby in one hand and bed-making with the other while calling out reassurance to the rest of the patients. In the room of one child the television was on, and there was Edwina

Currie making a remark to the effect that there wasn't a shortage of nurses. Sister says she found herself addressing the screen in no uncertain terms. I keep remembering that before we left the valley for the hospital the air force was daily whizzing through the sound barrier, skimming the bracken at a couple of million quid a throw. Being ill always seems to me a terrible waste of time unless you want a rest, but flying through the air in all that hardware practising for the next lot of hostilities – which would, in any event, see us all out, rendering even nurses redundant – seems a dreadful waste of money; especially when the planes crash in the bracken. I think I'm getting an *idée fix* about aeroplanes and conifers.

They've just taken the drip out of the daughter's arm, since she's managing to drink, and I feel faint. I'd make a hopeless nurse. We've both had to regress a few years. She needs some encouragement to swallow, so I grip her hand tightly, hold the cup to her mouth and say to the person who steals my tights and whose shoes are too big for me: 'One for Mummy, one for Daddy, one for Janet ... ' She takes it very well considering.

PS: Two fire engines have just drawn up outside the window.

Alarms and diversions

The daughter recovered miraculously quickly from glandular fever. The doctor was astonished to find her so well when she was taken to him for treatment after being thrown off a horse. I wasn't present at this accident and I am so glad. It sounds Wildly Western with horses bolting, feet caught in stirrups, the daughter being dragged, and people flying about in the air like so much popcorn. She was not badly hurt but is anti-horse at the moment, and my nerves are somewhat out of condition. What next, I ask myself, looking over my shoulder?

I spent last night alone here since everyone else has temporarily shot back to London to pick up the articles of clothing they couldn't live without for a second longer, or to see their best friend. I went to sleep at about 9 and woke up later to hear rain bucketing down and some ghosts talking in the kitchen below. I remembered quite positively that I had turned off the TV because it was boring, and I had the wireless in bed with me, silent. Nevertheless I wondered if I could possibly have turned the telly on again in a fit of absent-mindedness. I was not at that time in the least bit alarmed, merely wishing to ascertain whether the voices belonged to the TV or to ghosts. If the TV, I thought, it was incumbent on me to go downstairs and turn it off since I believe it is both expensive and a fire hazard to leave it on indefinitely. I felt about for the light switch and couldn't find it because, when it's dark in the country, it's good and dark; so I crawled out of bed and felt my way to the door – a matter of a foot or two. Then I got completely disoriented, and after I'd slapped the dressing-gown for being on the door when I didn't expect it I paused to consider. Hang on, I said to myself. What do you think you're doing crashing about in the middle of the night proposing to confront a roomful of ghosts? So I felt my way back to bed, got in and stayed there. Maybe it was just the rainwater gurgling through the mosses etc., but it sounded exactly like a number of men talking.

The night before I sat up until 3 am sipping Scotch and trying to learn Arabic. Akram taught me several useful words including the one for *tree*. The way I said it sounded a bit like *Cheshire* and we agreed hopelessly that I would probably go to my grave under the impression that the Arabic for tree is cheese. Abdul Hamid, who was Sultan when Akram's great-great etc. grandfather flourished, got annoyed with him and threatened to kill him by drowning him. The word for tying stones to people and chucking them in the ocean is *tabhir*, and I don't think we have a corresponding one. Lapidation is the translation of the word for throwing stones at people, and I was getting frustrated with the inadequacy of English when I learned that other languages have certain idlenesses in them too. For instance, the Turkish for Monday is the-day-after-Sunday, and for Saturday the-day-after-Friday. That does seem a little uninventive.

Next day when everyone had gone I heard a hooter in the garden and there was a Japanese on a scooter. He said he was a geologist from Cambridge and wanted to go and look at the stones in the stream, so I said it wasn't my stream but he could go anyway. I nearly despaired at the thought of all those foreigners who can talk perfect English and study their subjects in it while I, if I had crept down to listen to the ghosts, might have found they were talking in Welsh and wouldn't have been able to understand them – well, only a word or two – despite its being my native language. I intend to stay awake longer tonight and leave the door open an inch or two so that I'll be able to hear, and when I've got the time I'm going to learn to be a linguist.

September

Folly of tidying up

It's never happened to me before. It's not the sort of thing you expect. You take a taxi because the car's off the road. You don't ever imagine the taxi cab is going to break down. So there we were negotiating a roundabout on the way to Olympia and the taxi driver said the accelerator cable had become detached from whatever it's supposed to be attached to and we would have to pause while he had a little think about it. It was, of course, Bank Holiday Monday, yet another pimple on the face of time, and hence few garages were open.

The driver said bitterly that these things *only* happen on Bank Holiday Monday, and I had to agree with him, although in our case it's always the central heating on Christmas Eve or the washing machine on Maundy Thursday. He peered under the bonnet of his vehicle and then emerged to enquire if I had a bit of string about my person. He said he knew it was a silly question but he just wondered. As it happens, it wasn't such a silly question, because I had my handbag with me and in the normal way I'd probably have been able to provide him with yards of the stuff, only with Sod's Law once more in full majestic operation I had recently tidied my handbag. Ordinarily I could have supplied him with a pen-knife with a thing for taking stones out of horses' hooves, a catapult (this is not a flight of fancy: I found a catapult under my jumpers in the wardrobe just the other day), a number of fluffy sweets, possibly an old apple core, certainly about a million unanswered letters and receipts, and a few Deathless Thoughts scribbled down on bits of paper napkin etc.

As it was, I was unable to help. I did wonder wildly, as I got later and later for my appointment, whether I should emulate those screen heroines of the Civil War and tear my petticoat into strips. Then the driver dug out a length of ribbon, or possibly a frock belt, from the boot of his cab, and with a hoarse cry of satisfaction tied up his accelerator cable in such a fashion that we were able to limp onward. He was now driving by means of his brakes and gears. I didn't understand his explanation of our mode of progress, but the result was jerky. He said we'd be all right if we didn't encounter a hill. But we did: only a little one, since the terrain around Olympia is not unduly curvaceous, but a hill none the less. We went up it very slowly, and then, of course, all the roads in the way of my destination were closed for repairs, and both of us were reduced nearly to tears. Most of the other drivers on the road were rude and insensitive about our plight, perhaps not realising that we were in difficulties – though why, otherwise, they imagined we were crawling along at a senile snail's pace I can't think. Perhaps they thought I was taking an individual guided tour of the environs, and selfishly slowing down the traffic while appreciating the wildernesses of building sites and the forests of cones.

I went on thinking about tearing up petticoats as we travelled. It isn't as easy as it sounds. Once a piece of cloth has been hemmed you have to cut through the hem with scissors or rend it with your teeth. I was glad it hadn't been necessary as I visualised the scene: a mad lady by a spavined taxi cab frenziedly tearing up her clothing. It's taught me one thing – or rather reminded me of what I knew all the time. Tidying up is not the absolute virtue it is supposed to be. I threw away the catapult I found in the wardrobe, and already I'm regretting it.

When I finally reached my destination we sat in the garden and there were some very irritating pigeons flapping about just above our heads. Has anybody got a forked stick and a piece of elastic?

'A mad lady by a spavined taxi cab tearing up her clothes.'

Waste not, want not

We are still tidying up. I say 'still', but what I mean is we start doing it and are then so overwhelmed by the Augean-stable nature of the task that we have a cup of coffee and decide we'd better go and do some shopping. Contemplating the state of the whole house leads to despair. Every cupboard, every drawer, every corner needs sorting out. Even the jugs are full of old bills, and all the little bowls have keys in them. Nobody knows what locks these keys are supposed to open, but we don't dare throw them away in case there might be a locked box somewhere containing birth certificates and passports and one of the keys pertains to this efficient and mythical box. My system with documents and letters is usually to stuff them into the handbag of the moment until I can't close it any more and then I stuff that into the bottom of the wardrobe and buy a new one.

Janet made me haul them all out the other day, and I emptied them and put their contents into plastic bags and put those in the bottom of the wardrobe. Then I threw the handbags away. I don't know why this should seem tidier, but it does. Rearranging things gives me the illusion that one is tidying up. Alfie is preparing to ascend into the loft in order to make room for the pictures which occupy a sizeable alcove in my 'study'. I have never been in the loft because it gives me vertigo, but I have an idea of the state of it. There are prams up there and *papier mâché* baths for

babies and wicker cradles for them and boxes full of baby clothes and ball gowns in case our children have children and all these items might come in useful. There are boxes full of broken china waiting to be mended and trunks of old magazines and documents belonging to a lodger we once had who I think was a spy. I think this because he was a poet and rich, and that is unusual. He spent a lot of time lecturing to students in Communist countries and used Fortnums as his corner grocer shop. There are already a great many awful Victorian pictures of rosy-cheeked kiddies and big hairy dogs and angels. This is because once upon a time I couldn't resist buying them from the junk stall in the market simply because they cost sixpence. They are oddly sinister in the way that only the Victorians could achieve. You have the impression that the moment the artist put down his brush the dogs ate the children or the angels strangled them. There is one of two winsome little souls on the edge of a cliff with an angel behind them, clearly with the fixed intention of pushing them off. I don't think I ever meant to hang any of these pictures on the walls, so I must have been slightly unhinged when I bought them. There are old gas fires up there and nursery fenders and an iron thing to stand in the fireplace that Alfie's Mum threw out when *she* was tidying up. And there are curtains of cobwebs and carpets of dust and I expect there are dozens of spiders, alive and dead. We're going to hire a van and transport everything down to the country where there's another loft standing empty except for a few squirrels and maybe a ghost or two.

I had a nice letter from a lady in Holland to say that you could get rid of ghosts by politely asking them to leave, but I don't really want them to go. I find their presence rather flattering in the same way that one is flattered when bees visit the flowers in the garden. It makes me feel *accepted*. I was cross with Linda Mary for exorcising the ghost who was breathing at the back of the cottage and all the way up the mountain-side, but I mustn't be selfish. If it was an earthbound spirit and she returned it to the Lord, we can only rejoice. It's much tidier that way.

Alfie has just tidied up the vegetable rack in the kitchen. There was a very old potato in it with huge sprouts, so he's buried it in a flower pot in the back yard and perhaps we'll have new potatoes in time for Christmas. Anyone else would have thrown it away, but I have instilled in Alfie a sense of thrift. In a peculiar way untidiness and thrift go together. If you never waste anything, your dwelling place gets so crowded that in the end all that's left to do is throw yourself away. I'm not going to do that. I'm going to re-dispose everything and I'm not going to save old newspapers any more. Somewhere in the loft is a gadget for turning old newspapers into logs for the fire. I'm going to tell Alfie he can throw that away.

Birthday blues

I mostly forget anniversaries – or I try to. Too many are sorrowful and the others are a nuisance, necessitating awful, ghastly, boring frolicking and cries of 'Good Health' and 'Many Happy Returns'. At the absolutely worst – silver wedding anniversaries, for instance – people cannot be prevented from making speeches. Horror. As the housewife, I always find myself catering for these lowering occasions, and am therefore more than slightly resentful by the time the cake candles are lit. Also, having access to the cooking sherry, I am seldom in further need of liquid refreshment by the time the toasts are proposed. I'm ready for bed by then. We always sincerely forget our wedding anniversary. Someone says this is the sign of a happy marriage. Often, as a couple exchange red roses and a pair of silk socks, they are thinking – God, we've clocked up 30 years. How much *longer* ...?

It was my birthday on Wednesday and it passed fairly painlessly. We had a friend with us who had spent the night and at 8.30 am he expressed a desire for pints of bitter beer. He said he was going off to Smithfield on this quest, so I said to myself, What the hell, and went with him. At the first pub we approached we were refused entry. Our friend couldn't quite remember whether this was one of the establishments he was barred from, so we didn't argue but sped round the corner to a more accommodating hostelry. Here I demanded shandy, because I am not particularly fond of the taste of unadulterated beer, and our friend and the barman both nearly wept since they considered putting lemonade in it as some sort of sacrilege. They rolled their eyes and wrung their hands, and the barman flung in as little as possible, so that as the morning passed I ceased to mind about it being my birthday. There was a young man leaning on the bar gazing into his glass, and every so often he would remark: 'There she was, *gone*.' He would then follow this with 'I wandered lonely as a cloud', and I got the impression that he had just been deserted by some faithless female.

I asked him with womanly sympathy whether this was indeed the case and he said it was. His hands were sore too because he'd been digging a tunnel for a new underground route and he proved rather difficult to cheer up. Our friend assured him that there'd be another one along in a minute and I reminded him that men had died and worms had eaten them, but not for love; but he wouldn't be consoled.

There was a momentary distraction when we noticed an unattended briefcase leaning against a bar stool, and handed it to the barman. 'Don't shake it,' he screamed. I'd forgotten the days when we were constantly adjured not to mess with unexplained suitcases and plastic bags but to alert the station/shop/bar staff, leave the premises quietly and wait for the bomb squad. I suppose fashions in death change as much as everything else.

We bade farewell to our young acquaintance with the calloused hands and the broken heart because I had a luncheon engagement and my friend was due in Grantchester. The fellow was reluctant to see us go and if I hadn't had the dashes of lemonade in the lager I daresay I'd have taken him with me. One can get very fond of the people one meets in bars. The trouble is they then appear sort of different in the daylight and you realise that taking them with you is rather like taking a goldfish for a walk: not entirely correct, and surprising for the next people you run into.

I had a delicious lunch and drifted home replete with *noisette* of lamb. Then I think I had a little sleep, and in the evening some of us went out to our pet Chinese restaurant for supper. This is, of course, the only way to handle anniversaries. Everyone in the family would prefer to dine at Cheng Du rather than watch Mummy getting red in the face with rage and standing over a hot stove and knocking back the sparkling white – if it's got bubbles in, people think it's festive – and refusing to eat any dinner because she's bored with cooking it. Deirdre has just rung to say she may be in Ireland until December and what are we going to do about Christmas. I think I am going to run straight round to Cheng Du and ask them what *they're* going to do for Christmas. We may be spending it together.

Cat brought in

This is for the attention of Matthew who is currently travelling round Ireland (or maybe he's gone somewhere else by now) talking to people about cats. I want him to know that Puss is perfectly well and living again in London.

Matthew is compiling a book about people and their pussy cats and wished to include Puss and me. So we went off to the country so that she could be photographed in pleasantly rural surroundings. She was as good as gold for the camera and sat on my knee watching the birdie; she posed on the stairs like any movie goddess; she presented her best profile and stared straight at the lens, although admittedly she refused to be portrayed in the front doorway – we don't know why. Then when the time came to go home the stupid mog disappeared up the mountainside. Furious yells of 'Puss, you blasted cat, where are you, you disastrously dumb animal' produced no result. You know what cats are. In the end we had to come home without her, having asked Celia in the shop if her son Adam would nip up daily and feed her until somebody found time to race back down the motorway and pick her up. I *knew* she'd be all right really, but that didn't prevent me from lying awake thinking about ferrets and weasels and monster owls and mad dogs and gamekeepers who claim that cats eat little pheasants. They do, of course, because pheasants are not merely remarkably thick, they are barely capable of lifting themselves off the ground. On the other hand cats also catch baby rabbits, which should make gamekeepers cheerful. After a few days the third son bowled off and collared her – so that's all right. I know Matthew was worrying about it because he sent a card to say so. I owe an awful lot of letters and I can't find my envelopes.

I was reminded again of Wales the other day. I was whinging about having to go from West to North London on the train because I suspected it would be full of rapists and muggers travelling round in pursuit of their horrid trade. I wasn't really nervous, you understand. I just felt like whining a bit, so that's what I whined about. The friend who was escorting me to the station had clearly had enough of it so, calling my bluff, he seized upon another solitary lady and asked her how far she was going. She obviously thought that *her* expected rapist or mugger had materialised and took a step back, eyes narrowed. Hastily I reassured her that all was well and my friend was merely manifesting a disinterested if faintly insincere concern for our safety, whereupon she spoke in the accents of my native heath. 'You're Welsh,' I observed brilliantly. When she agreed that this was so I asked her where she came from and she said 'Bangor', so I said I'd been to school there and she said so had she and then we had one of those 'do you remember' conversations about Miss Smart and Miss Featherstone and Miss Lawford and Miss Reeves, so the escorting friend went off and left us to it.

This type of chat is undeniably of less interest to the outsider than it is to the participants. I made another friend in the quarter of an hour we were on the train. She had four good sons and a little daughter who was driving her *mad*. Coincidences, coincidences. I met no more muggers than Puss had met ferrets and I am going off to light a candle to the legion of guardian angels.

October

Chicken and egg

A week of minor – but none the less infuriating for that – crises. Janet is off on her hols and I've been flying round London on buses. I hate those ones with automatic doors and just a driver who demands the correct amount of money, because I never seem to have it. And I can't find my clothes. I wonder if the tinkers took them. And I was rinsing a chicken's giblets under the tap the other day when its stomach leapt out of the sieve and down the overflow. The final straw is always something trivial like that. I poked round for it with a dry-cleaner's coat-hanger and contemplated stuffing the cat down after it, but it's still down there somewhere. I was going to give it to the cats anyway, because no one else wanted it, but I don't like to think of it down there. Alan Bennett came rushing in yesterday for the plumber's telephone number because he had a flood, and I wondered for a mad moment if the chicken's stomach could be causing it.

I ran out of dishwashing powder one evening when the shops were shut and the dishwasher was full of dirty plates, and I mislaid *The Moonstone* when I was in the middle of it. I found it again, but by then I'd forgotten the plot up to the point I'd stopped reading. I don't mind forgetting the plot when I've got to the end, but while reading is in progress I like to keep the hang of the thing. I have letters to write and forms to fill in, and I should be cooking wholesome meals, but I am so sick of cooking that my brain refuses to divulge the information necessary to assemble the ingredients. I have to go plodding round the market looking at the stuff on the stalls and in the shops to remind myself of the things that people eat. Aubergines and swedes and plums are three foodstuffs I'd forgotten about; fresh mackerel and pickled tongue are two more. I used to make cassoulets, and stuffed breast of lamb and junket flavoured with rose-water, but now I don't, although I did throw together a casserole the other day with leeks and mushrooms and the chicken whose stomach went down the overflow. I do wish I could forget about *that*. I can remember all the worrying things, but nothing useful. Marks & Spencers is no help. Now we no longer have any proper dairy or grocer's shop in the district we buy our milk and butter there, and even if I could remember where they are kept the management keeps moving them. Each trip out for dairy produce takes on the air of a safari as we track the semi-skimmed to its latest lair.

And while we're on the subject can anyone tell me why it's so difficult to find fresh eggs? Milk comes fresh, and fruit and veg and meat. Why not eggs? Maybe one yolk out of six will sit on its little cushion of white, but the rest slither all over the place: not rotten, but not in the first flush of youth. Nothing makes me crosser than a poached egg broken in the water, or a fried egg in the bacon fat. I am tempted to keep a chicken or two in the back-yard. Alfie's Mum used to have a couple in Kentish Town, but they went off the lay and she couldn't bear to have them killed. This story has a sad ending, but I've forgotten what it is, and Alfie's away in the cottage, so I can't ask him. I'd telephone him but the bell usually doesn't ring down there and when he didn't answer I'd imagine he'd fallen off the mountain and I'd worry. Even in the country when Mr Christmas's chickens are off the lay we have to rely on supermarket eggs, and everything is looking rather bleak. It is particularly inconvenient, as omelettes and convent eggs and soufflés are some of the things I can remember. I just said to the first-born son, would he care for an egg for lunch? He said he hadn't looked an egg in the face since he was nine years old. I'd forgotten that.

Unspeakable goings on

To the Groucho Club – referred to by Someone as 'the unacceptable face of publishing' – for a party to celebrate Caroline's book about hunting, *In the Pink*. The hunting community had got wind of this work and, suspecting that it might not be a total eulogy of their pastime, had been wildly trying to track her down to serve an injunction on her. They couldn't find her. I suppose if she'd been a fox they'd have managed it, but looking through directories for an address is clearly more complicated than pounding through field and covert sitting on a horse. I was rather disappointed not to find a group of mounted MFHs waving their whips outside the Coach and Horses, but the party was jolly. I wore my aggressively nylon snow-leopard coat as a rebuke to anyone around who might be in sympathy with blood sports, and the third son wore the jacket of my cerise satin trouser-suit because it is more supremely pink than anything you've ever seen. The definition of 'pink' led to some very startling colour clashes since Caroline and some others came in hunting pink and everyone else was led astray by the word into powder or shocking pink. Anyway, Caroline says the upper classes don't say 'pink' any more because the *hoi polloi* have caught on. Now they say *red* coats, which makes them sound like Butlins cheer-leaders.

There was a poor stuffed fox in the middle of the room wearing the hunted expression customary to foxes and I wondered if this look was genetic or required. People have been chasing his tribe for so long I suppose it could be either. Caroline's book is fair and balanced but I finished it with the impression that certain sorts of English persons would rather chase foxes than anything – than go to war or to church or make love or look after the children or eat or drink or *anything* – that chasing foxes comes before Queen, Country and the Family, and that a life not spent in the saddle is a life wasted. I find it odd. I would rather do almost anything than get up early in the cold and spend all day risking my neck flying round the countryside on the back of some nag. I think it is yet another addiction, a means of setting the adrenalin coursing, and once hooked it is difficult to find a cure. One poor man in the book suddenly came to his senses after a lifetime of hunting and asked himself what on earth he was doing, pursuing foxes all the time. He voiced this feeling, and all the other hunters turned on him with the sort of bitter loathing most of us reserve for rapists or child abusers. He almost had to change his name. Caroline also reveals that foxes are sometimes specially bred, or caged until their moment comes – something the huntsmen have passionately denied.

The Rt. Hon. The Earl of Wilton PC, GCH, DCL etc. writing in 1868 says: 'In this country [he is being superior here about the Continent] foxes are preserved especially for the sport they afford. Otherwise they are mere vermin, and care is taken even to keep up the breed for the purpose. It is this especially that marks the difference between the English and all other people; it is not the mere brutal passion for killing, but a real love for a manly and exciting diversion – the islander's birthright: giving health and strength, yet not altogether divested of that amount of peril in the pursuit, which in the true sportsman adds to its charm.'

I can't follow that. Can anyone follow that? Tally Ho.

Stage fright

As Someone remarked yesterday, 'It is quite easy to be natural, but fearfully difficult to pretend to be natural.' This was *apropos* of Home Life at the moment, as we have been joined by a camera crew. It is notably difficult, I have discovered, to open one's wardrobe with every appearance of unconcern and a straight face when one's instinct is telling one to totter back, hands raised crying 'Alack-a-day, Gadzooks' or 'Shiver me timbers' or 'Angels and Ministers of Grace defend us – there's a cameraman in my wardrobe'. You're not supposed to know he's in there. Someone is actually rather good. He said 'Hello, darling' about a million times yesterday with seeming spontaneity, whereas I, after marching out of the gate five times, found I was thinking so hard about it, and to such little purpose, that I'd almost forgotten how to put one foot in front of the other. P. said by the time I'd finished I should be rather good at it, but it doesn't work like that. David up at the old Piano Factory says anyway that's nothing. When Hitchcock made *Frenzy* at Duckworth's old offices in Covent Garden one chap had merely to lean out of the window and enquire of another chap in the street below, 'What's the odds on Tweetie Pie for the 3.30?', while the chap below responded '30 to 1' or something, and it took them all day.

Then I watched some Cecil B. de Mille on telly. A disciple arriving late for the Last Supper struck a chord in me. I could just hear the director saying, 'Look left *slowly*, then look right. *Don't* look at the camera – *don't* look at me. *Cut* – right, we'll try that one *again*.' I bet that disciple was carried off the set in a state of nervous exhaustion. It is also very difficult to pretend you're sitting by yourself in a taxi cab gazing pensively out of the window when there are three people with cameras and related objects squashed in the back with you and another one crouching in the front by the driver.

Jemma had a much harder time, I have to admit. She's been in a horror film working from dawn to dusk having her eyebrows singed by flame throwers and getting soaked in synthetic blood. And she had to run upstairs time and again carrying a small grown-up until she sank to her knees and couldn't move another step. She said she burst into tears several times and got shouted at, which seems unfair. It is customary to attempt to dissuade people from going on the stage: 'Do you realise the amount of sheer hard work, pain, heartbreak and rejection involved?' The aspiring actor traditionally responds to this in the affirmative, eyes glowing with divinely inspired ardour. Then the first person says, 'If you must – so be it', and sighs, and assumes an expression of mingled compassion, approval and misgiving, and the aspiring actor exits stage-left, looking raptly upwards, breaking into a little run and possibly raising her (it's usually a her) arms, and there's some music and the first person shakes his head with a tender and rueful smile. Then there follows a lot of sheer hard work, pain, heartbreak and rejection until the moment of triumph with bright lights, standing ovations and furs and jewels, and then it's heartbreak and rejection time again with ruined relationships, professional jealousy and dirty work and the demon drink and a few suicide attempts.

In real life the actors I know live rather solid and balanced lives, carefully investing their money, and knitting in the intervals when they're not required to do their bit. Nevertheless I would rather sell melons myself. The business seems to me to be compounded of boredom and terror in equal measure. I can't even just watch with equanimity. When Beryl's Rudi was in a play at the National she had to scamper along a 9ft-high wall and I didn't see her do it because I had my fingers crossed and stuck in my eyes. I can only thank Providence that none of us is involved in any chariot races.

Mother knows best

A few weeks ago I dreamed that I was in a violently swaying house. I thought it might have been because there had just been an earthquake in L.A. and the fourth son is out there. He says he lives in a quake-proof house 'built on rubber bands or something', but I was not entirely reassured. Now I think it was yet another case of pre-cognition and I knew the hurricane was coming. Patrice knew it too. Her son was due to sail on the

Newhaven-Dieppe ferry and she implored him to postpone the trip.

'Why Mum?' he enquired. 'It blowing or something? High waves anywhere?'

She had to admit that at the moment all seemed calm, but she was deeply uneasy.

In the end he was flung about at sea for eight hours instead of four, and the moral is 'Always listen to your Mum'. The people in the harbour at Newhaven said the passengers in that boat now knew what hell was. Patrice says so does she. She sat listening to the winds baying all night and she still doesn't feel very well.

I was in Wales when the storms hit London and back in London when they hit Wales. I rather enjoyed listening to the weather forecasters having trouble with their tenses – 'It may be rather windy', 'It is being very windy', 'It has been *extremely* windy' – but the damage was disheartening to see. As we drove into London I felt like General Paton or somebody in a film approaching the devastation of a war-torn city when the enemy had been vanquished. Our Tree of Heaven was a casualty – not surprisingly since its roots do not go deep and we've lost previous ones in other, less violent storms – but the garden looks as though it has had a penitential haircut, like a prisoner, and we will have to plant yet another sumac (its proper name) and wait a month or two for it to leap up to its full height. They do grow fast, but then they keep falling over. On the other hand if they were immemorial elms or stately oaks they'd have flattened the dwelling place or the neighbour's Porsche, so I think I'll stay with the arboreal weeds.

Alfie had a different problem when he was in the country. He came back last week and telephoned the minute he got into his flat. Either we have a new ghost down there or the one we already had has changed his mode. Most of us have heard him banging, but usually by day. Alfie fell thankfully into bed one night after a day of pony-trekking and was just about to go off into a dreamless sleep when he heard the ghost go *boing*. He crept to the window and put his ear against the opening at the top. This, he claims, was very brave because by now the ghost was going *boing-boing-boing* at measured, regular intervals. Why, I asked, didn't Alfie go out and ask him what he was doing? Alfie uttered a hoarse, incredulous laugh down the line. He said the noise was coming from the barn and nothing on God's earth would have persuaded him to go anywhere near it. He had closed the window and leapt back into bed, too frightened even to go to the other room and wake his sister-in-law so she could hear it too.

I was rather cross with him, because nobody ever believes in the ghost and another witness (or do I mean auditor?) would have lent credibility to our claims. I think our house may be a sort of pull-up for ghosts, an inn for spectres, because they all do different things. One does the *boinging*, one does the breathing, and some talk by themselves in the house. One, Alfie maintains, makes the end room in the other barn go very very cold. I'm not in the least afraid of any of them, and Alfie's friend Jean says being in our bit of the country is like sitting in God's lap. There used to be a nunnery there and the saint who ran the place was granted the right of sanctuary in perpetuity by Brochwel Ysgythrog, Prince of Powys, so clearly evil spirits would not feel particularly at home there. I think there must be something amiss with Alfie's conscience and I'm going to have a word with him about it. Or perhaps he was just dreaming.

November

Sucks to Mrs Beeton

I was sitting in Cheng Du at lunchtime the other day waiting for my companion to arrive as arranged. And waiting. The third son who was also expected was at home also waiting – for his hair or his shirt to dry, I think. I get bored sitting by myself in restaurants. Even other people's conversations need two eavesdroppers, just as ghosts need two witnesses. Other people's conversations are sometimes quite unbelievable and as you recount them your audience assumes that sceptical expression which makes you start shouting 'It's true, I tell you. True *true*!' After a while I requested the waiter to telephone the son and tell him to get a move on. All around me customers were tucking into the Szechuan prawns and the black bean sauce and I wanted to hasten through the various courses until I could get to the banana fritters which are my current passion.

When the son finally arrived and the other expected companion had not I had an inspiration. It was Friday but I hadn't yet read my *Spectator*. 'Nip round to the newsagent,' I said, 'and buy another copy. Set the sales figures soaring.' Turning to the end, I read, 'Jeffrey Bernard will be back next week'. A week is a long time to wait, so we ordered. Then we thought we might as well make a party out of it, so we telephoned the fifth son and invited him too.

It has taken many years for me to eat in restaurants without a sense of guilt. In some establishments I still have misgivings as to the standards of hygiene behind the scenes, but Cheng Du positively sparkles with cleanliness and I'd rather have lunch there than a bacon sandwich in my own kitchen. It is very near to home and so there are no problems with transport, and in my opinion Cheng Du is the brightest spot on the face of the rapidly changing Camden Town. Once upon a time the choice of restaurants was limited. Quite a few Greek, one Chinese, one Italian and assorted Greasy Spoons. Now they range from French and German to Japanese and at the weekend you can graze on all manner of exotic delicacies from wayside stalls – kebabs and samosas and chou chou and tempura: a welcome change from hamburgers and hot dogs and surely healthier. You can watch them being prepared and not have to worry that the chef may not be concentrating because he's too busy jumping on the cockroaches or chasing a rat along the draining board. My prejudices about eating out are not dead, and I still recommend that people choose a simple grill rather than the made dishes which in the past have certainly harboured the scrapings from other diners' plates.

Diana Melly relates that she once knew a place where yesterday's Spaghetti Bolognese was today's Minestrone. I have to admit that I do that sort of thing at home – left-over fish pie is transformed into fish cakes, roast lamb into moussaka and pork into rissoles – but this is thriftily traditional and permissible in the housewife. One does not expect to pay through the nose for second-hand food when splashing out in a restaurant.

I have just remembered that it is some time since I visited L'Amandier where I fly through the first course in order to get to the *crème brulée*, so when Jeff comes back he may well find me there. Otherwise I might be strolling along the High Street with a hunk of pitta bread. I won't be in my pinny stirring the *soupe bonne femme*. My outlook is becoming more Parisian and Mrs Beeton can go and boil her head.

Sucks again

There's a cobweb on our bedroom ceiling. Only one, I hasten to assure you. It hangs near a window and I get up late every morning because I like to lie in bed watching it drifting in the draught. Sometimes it reminds me of the Queen Mother, its only purpose in life being to wave.

Each day I picture myself or, more likely, Alfred tackling it with a special cobweb-remover such as every good housewife used to keep in the broom-cupboard together with her carpet-beater, feather duster and similar redundant domestic aids. Then when I get up I forget all about it. Mrs Beeton would be disgusted with me. She said bedrooms had to be swept every day, the windows opened and the bedclothes aired. You had to sprinkle damp tea-leaves on the carpet before sweeping it so the dust would adhere to them, and once a week you had to scrub the floorboards with hot water and soda. What a drag. She assumed of course that all respectable households included a maid or two, or at least a cook-general, but I don't think cooks-general ever ventured upstairs. They were too busy blacking the range and blowing it into life in preparation for the enormous breakfasts the Victorians required before they faced the day. Then they had to cope with the butcher and the baker and the milkman, and render down the dripping so they could sell it as one of 'cook's perks', and boil Spotted Dick for pudding after lunch while thinking about the Nesselrode for pudding after dinner. Cook had very little time for general housework, so I imagine the lady of the small household had to do it herself. At the same time she had to maintain a neat appearance and keep her temper. No Lady was ever seen out of countenance, certainly not when the servants were around – even if it was only Cook.

You have to admire the Victorians a little bit, if only because they did all the housework without a vacuum cleaner. The vacuum cleaner has changed the face of civilisation. I don't need a special thing with extending poles to get that cobweb. All I have to do, if I could only remember to do it, is point the nozzle of the vacuum cleaner at it, and whoosh – a pure and unsullied ceiling. The only thing you can't do with a hoover is clean the bath or your teeth or the lavatory pan. Once upon a time before everybody had a hoover the women's magazines used to devote column after column to tips on how to clean up the home. Now all they tell you is how to arrange the flowers – 'a discarded Wellington boot makes an amusing centre-piece, filled with autumn branches and fronds of Old Man's Beard ... '; or how to apply the latest eye-make-up, avoid those tell-tale signs of ageing and achieve multiple orgasm.

The extraordinary thing is that although I cordially detest housework, even with a hoover, I don't find the current magazines anything like as interesting as the old ones. I am fascinated to learn that a solution of boiled ivy

'A solution of boiled ivy leaves
will take the shine out of the seat
of your husband's pants.'

leaves will take the shine out of the seat of your husband's pants; that a dash of methylated spirits in the washing water will put a shine on your windows; that potato water is excellent for cleaning carpets and rugs, and that if their colours have faded they can be freshened by sponging with a mixture of one part ox-gall to two parts water. Our carpets have to content themselves with a good hoovering since I can't imagine where one would now obtain ox-gall. From an ox, I suppose.

I am exercised about these questions at the moment because Alfred, the hoover-wielder, has not arrived and I'm damned if I'm going to do it myself. Zélide's brother, Micky, tells me that Quentin Crisp has a theory about dust. If you leave it for four years it doesn't matter any more. It seems to stabilise itself and the quantity appears not to increase. Whereas if you keep hoovering it up it comes back and you have to do it again. Rather like answering letters – if you do, your correspondent does it again and you go into perpetual motion. I am just going to sit here watching the dust settle until Alfie appears, and when he does I think I'll tell him to ignore the cobweb. I like watching it floating about. It's restful. God save the Queen Mother.

Street foolish

I may have remarked before that I seldom venture out of Camden Town. I now realise that this is because it is hardly possible to venture out of Camden Town. One could take the tube to the wider world, I suppose, but I'm not going to. Beryl had to go on the Northern Line the other morning because she couldn't get a cab and she said it was *hell*. One day, again due to the absence of cabs, she had to come home on a Hoppa and she didn't like that either. There are too many other people going back and forth by these means. Some of them are robbers and some are mad, and they're all in too great a hurry to mind whether they walk on your feet or push you off the platform or under the bus.

Last week I was invited to lunch at the Gay Hussar, not a million miles away from here. That'll make a pleasant change, I thought, accepting with alacrity. While we're at it, I said to myself, we may as well deliver some books to a venue in Central London where they were required. I informed Janet of this plan and said she could drive me, thus saving cab fares. It was pissing down with rain and she said dubiously that the roads would be congested but if we set off in good time we should make it eventually. Some hours later we realised that I might, with my luck, arrive at the Gay Hussar in time for tea, or possibly just hit the cocktail hour. Then as the skies grew ever darker and we sat amidst the stationary cars, lorries and buses we decided to sod the whole thing and go home. I had a dryish cheese roll for a late lunch instead of whatever they were having at the Gay Hussar and after that I watched the end of *Gaslight* on telly, occasionally glancing out of the window at the increasing gale bending what remains of the trees in the neighbours' gardens and reflecting that it was perhaps just as well some of these trees had fallen over and squashed some of the parked cars because one or two more vehicles on the roads would have brought the metropolis to a total standstill.

When we were stuck just outside Trafalgar Square Janet whiled away the time by describing some of the landmarks.

'Parisians can direct a stranger to the Deux Magots with no trouble at all...'

I've never liked London so I've never learned much about it. I've been to Trafalgar Square before and to Buckingham Palace, and I've looked at the Houses of Parliament and I knew Downing Street was out there somewhere – and Scotland Yard – but I couldn't have taken you to any of these famous sites or told you where they were in relation to each other. I still couldn't, but I am now at least aware that the top of Big Ben is visible from wherever we were – the end of the Strand I think. There was a church in the middle of the road. Janet says it's one of Wren's, but even she isn't absolutely certain.

This extraordinary ignorance of the city one lives in is surely unusual. Parisians can direct the stranger to the *Deux Magots* with no trouble at all, Florentines know their Florence and when I lived in Liverpool I could have quartered the place blindfold. London is perhaps too big, and poorly signposted. I used to know Chelsea quite well but I recently got off the 31 bus on to which I had climbed in a fit of bravado, found myself at the World's End and walked round in a huge circle before arriving at my intended destination – about two minutes' walk from the World's End if one had only been concentrating and the street signs had been clearer. Some of this lack of interest in one's surroundings is due to the hopeless feeling that faceless and ruthless powers are in control – local councils for the most part – ripping up the paving stones at random, closing down the little shops and authorising the erection of nightmarish mega-stores. There was a criminal lunatic around at one time who proposed to drive a motorway smack through the Old Piano Factory, but happily he ran out of funds. I seem to remember he had a beard, and this intended motorway was his most passionately favourite thing in life. The disappearance of the few landmarks one does recognise under building sites, tower blocks and roads makes it even more difficult to find one's way home. I went into a pub by one door the other evening, came out by a different one and thought I'd fallen into something by Kafka. The ABC building has disappeared, Camden Road is unrecognisable and I could have been in Outer Mongolia for all I knew. Plotting a course by the stars and guided by the smell of rotting vegetable matter I made my way to the familiar market and so to bed. They intend to abolish the street market, and if they do I'll be utterly lost.

Janet suggests putting curtains in the car and installing a coffee machine and some bookshelves since she spends so much time just sitting in it. Then it won't matter if we get lost. Our address will be Stationary Vehicle somewhere in the Strand on the way to the Gay Hussar.

Dogged by misfortune

Poor Alfie had a rough time recently. He was minding a house while its owners were away and it turned against him in the way of a child left in the care of a stranger. First the phone rang, so he flew upstairs and sat in a chair to answer it. 'The Whatnot Residence … ' he began elegantly in the best of his selection of telephone manners – and the chair collapsed beneath him. It is difficult to be elegant lying flat on your back amidst the debris of another person's chair. The combined sensations of shock, wrath, indignity and guilt make coherence impossible. When he'd recovered sufficiently he went downstairs to feed the dogs and the dog bowl slipped from his nerveless fingers and broke in half.

'What sort of dogs?' I asked inconsequentially.

'The embarrassing sort,' said Alfie gloomily. 'The sort when you take them out for a walk people look at them, and then they look at you.'

He had more trouble with the dogs. They fell out over

dinner and fought ferociously round his ankles, and now he says he won't just have to brush them, he'll have to wash them to get the blood out of their fur. He asked whether I thought he should hoover through the house, or whether that might seem a little pointed, an implicit criticism of the state of the place, and I advised against it. The way his luck was running the hoover might have accidentally swallowed the dogs.

The curse followed him here. I had bought a pair of ear-rings for a friend and left them on the kitchen table roughly wrapped in the plastic film with bubbles in it which children like to pop. After Alfie had tidied the table I couldn't find them. I asked the daughter if she'd pinched the plastic to play with and she denied it – she is 14 and I had to admit her bubble-popping days were past. I concluded that Alfie must have mistaken the package for rubbish and slung it away in a black bag. The next step, of course, was to ferret through the black bags and see if it was there. I spent Sunday doing that. I emptied all three of the bags on to newspaper on the kitchen floor and surveyed the detritus of the recent past spread before my eyes: most unpleasant, but something of a revelation. Hair combings, fag ends, tea bags, potato peelings, and the outside leaves of lettuce formed, as it were, the mulch. Then there were old milk cartons, cat food tins and a surprising number of empty bottles. There were piles of old newspapers damp with deliquescence, dozens of crumpled tissues and discarded wrappers from biscuit packets, sausages etc., hundreds of plastic carrier bags, which surprised me as I have hundreds more waiting in a cupboard to come in useful (who throws them away?), and a perfectly ghastly corpse bag containing the heads, skin and bones of two salmon trout. There was also a bundle of kitchen paper, but I don't think I'll tell you what was in that. Or perhaps I'd better, in case you think it was even worse than it was. The cat had been sick, you see. Oh God.

Something in this exercise led me to meditate on sin. I thought of the soul of the recently dead person being emptied on to the floor of heaven so the angels could riffle through it (holding their noses) to see if there was anything good in it. I didn't find the ear-rings, which was dispiriting, and while the experience undoubtedly had its salutary aspects it left me feeling melancholy and in immediate need of a good bath, followed by a rush to confession. I forgave Alfie for throwing away this expensive gift because he really couldn't be blamed and then I found it tucked away between the jugs on a shelf in the back kitchen. *I* didn't put it there, and he says he didn't, and it wasn't there when I first looked so I don't know what happened. I put it down to the angels.

December

Cardboard Christmas

Christmas is coming. I don't know how the goose is getting on and I don't care either, but the Scotch is appearing again warmly wrapped up in CARDBOARD BOXES.

I hate cardboard boxes. I hate them with a bitter, twisted, inverted passion that can't be doing me any good. The third son came back from an evening's shopping recently bearing a carrier bag and wearing a little wry smile. He watched me as he put a gold and scarlet box on the table, and I think my reaction was all that he could have wished. There is something smug about cardboard boxes, something over-protective, something nanny-like and overbearing, something patronising and ineffably annoying. Something that drives one to drink. These seasonal Gift Packages are the absolute worst, the outside edge, the inky bottom. Why should items that one buys the year round suddenly turn up in fancy dress? Eh? Answer me that. I'll tell you why. It's because the manufacturers think we're all *stupid*. That's why. They have a (card)board meeting every year, and a chap of generous *embonpoint* with a watch chain on it sticks his thumbs in his waistcoat, leans back a little, and says 'Christmas is here again, fellow directors. Now Mrs Average-Idiot in the street out there won't have realised this, so we'll point it out to her. She'll have no idea of what to give as presents even when it's dawned on her, so we'll give her a good hard nudge in the ribs, and we'll Gift-Wrap our product and adorn it with robins and holly leaves and Daddy Christmas, and *then* she'll know what to do.' I often give my friends bottles of Scotch and I'm perfectly capable – or at least Janet is – of wrapping them up in festive tissue. I'm not about to send them through the post, dammit, so why put them in that infuriating armour which makes the Boxing Day (Boxing?) garbage-disposal problem even worse?

Two of my hatreds run together here. I detest conifer plantations, and I suspect they turn the nasty things into cardboard boxes. Apparently the trees that form those endless combed rows which deform most of the countryside are good for nothing but pulp; so the people who get government grants to plant them and income-tax relief when they sell them are largely responsible for the hideous proliferation of cardboard boxes. If the trees have to be sold to make cardboard, then the cardboard has to be sold to make boxes. And who pays for the privilege of being buried in redundant packaging? You and me.

Yet another of my hatreds was involved in this festering mélange of prejudice last week: *Blue Peter*. I never watch *Blue Peter* because the unworthy hope that the girl swarming down the skyscraper will throttle herself in her abseiling rope is not an emotion of which I am proud. I do not enjoy the vicarious embarrassment of watching eager young people projecting their personality at the wrong camera, or speaking the spontaneous lines which each had arranged the other would say. Their little garden annoys me, and their good works are a depressing contemporary manifestation of the efforts of Lady Bountiful Muck: 'Now come on children. I'm sure we all want to help those who are less fortunate than ourselves.' But one day, asleep in front of the telly, I woke to the sight of a girl torturing cardboard boxes. Instead of switching over to the snooker I watched with perverted glee as she mutilated a cereal box, a suet box, and a toothpaste box. It was like one of those tasteless Roman gladiatorial spectacles where lions and bears and wild boars bite bits off each other. She covered all those helpless boxes with decorated paper, stuck them together and advised the youth of the country to do likewise and offer them as gifts to their big sister, their Mum or their Aunty. They could be used, she informed us, either as make-up or sewing boxes. I don't suppose anyone will actually do it because their Mum, if she's got any sense, won't let them make all that mess, but I do hope the daughter or my niece (luckily I haven't got a little sister) weren't watching. Presented with one of these ghastly artefacts by a loving child you'd have to use it. It would lie around taking up space for the rest of your life, and when you died you'd have to take it with you.

I wonder how long it will be before the pressure of the pulp industry and big business forces us all (remember the wool trade and shrouds) to be really truly literally buried in cardboard boxes.

Ruined castle

I'm writing this on the train (BR) – 15 minutes late. The one down was late too. Object on the line. Someone tells me that the word is used here entirely correctly – in the sense of something thrown in the way. How very educated of the guard who relayed this frustrating information. But I wish they wouldn't be so delicate in their descriptions. It leaves one consumed with morbid curiosity – what sort of object? Cow? Body? Cardboard box?

I had to wait for hours at Llandudno Junction for a taxi to turn up before we drove through the night to the coastal watering place where I was reared. The route is dreadfully untidy on account of the four-lane highway they're in the course of constructing. It looks as though millions of mindless moles had been at work, and the local ambience will not be improved when it's completed. It shears along the shore line which, while not unspoiled (there are caravan sites along it and the sort of council housing which only Celtic councils seem able to produce), was not entirely ruined. It is now. I kept remembering the Heir to the Throne, whose principality this is, and wondering what he would make of it. Conway Castle is nice. If I'd been him I'd have had it repaired and redecorated and lived in it myself, but as it happens it would've been a mistake since the motorway will now be roaring round it and he wouldn't have got a wink of sleep. Actually the motorway may be going underground there, or underwater – it isn't very clear – so subsidence may well turn out to be the problem. In any event the view is going to lack the *je ne sais quoi* it once had. Along the whole of the littoral the view is going to lack that. I've never really been able to work out why the coast road is so congested. Where is everybody going? After a very short while you get to Bangor and Caernarvon, and after that to Anglesey and Holyhead. I wondered for a trice if it was the Irish going home, but it can't be that because they're all still in Camden Town. Whoever they were I shouldn't think they'll be going anywhere in future since whatever charm the coast possessed has now gone. They can't all have been on business bent. There isn't all that much business west of Penmaenmawr. Maybe they were mostly coming the other way.

I wonder if the Prince of Wales knows. I, together with many of my contemporaries, have been inclined to republicanism ever since our mothers made us listen to the then Princesses Elizabeth and Margaret Rose on Children's Hour, commiserating with us on being parted from our loved ones, and piping 'Good night children everywhere.' They wore white socks and their hair was neatly curled and they were held up to us as role models. Most of us of whatever sex had a tendency to identify with William, Henry, Douglas and Ginger and not with Violet Elizabeth, so this instilled in us a certain resentment. Much later I flew into a rage and tore Someone's invitation to a Buckingham Palace Garden Party into little bits because the Prince had said something half-witted about the Roman Church not letting Prince Michael marry what's-her-face with full rite and ceremony. However, since then the Heir has come a long way and I find his views on almost everything perfectly sound – i.e. similar to my own – and I could almost lie down and die for King and Country when he's rude about architects (known round here as "eartattacks'). I say awful things about them myself but nobody listens. I've been saying for years that the whole profession should be discouraged from practising – by force if need be – until they learn to get it right. How wonderful to be in the position of future Ruler and tell the Visigoths what you think of them. How even more delightful if they mind – and some of them, at least, must. I do hope he sticks to his guns when he succeeds to the throne and refuses to give any of them knighthoods or those honours that are signified by letters after the name.

ARIBA is enough to distinguish them from the rest of the human race and they should be avoided like the plague. Just look at what they've done. *Si monumentum requiris*, as they say.

Creation myths

I have a kind of alien living in my semi-conscious like a mite in cheese. He emerges early in the mornings before I'm properly awake and gives me peculiar advice and instructions: nothing useful like 'Remember, it's six and three quarters shopping days to Christmas', or 'You forgot to put the cat out last night', or 'You left your reading glasses on the third shelf in the pantry', but *strange* things. The other morning he was gibbering at me through the mists of sleep, insisting that I write a story about two archetypal characters called Dumbeau and Dumbelle. It was to be a creation myth. Then I woke up and he retired backstage leaving me to work out the details. I did start on this story, but it's not the sort of thing that really interests me, so I shall have to wait for the mite to return with the full idea.

I hope he leaves it till after Christmas, about which I have been unusually neglectful – i.e. I haven't started worrying about it yet. I'm usually in a state of collapse by December 15 but I am growing blasé. Janet has been plodding round acquiring presents – mostly knitted things, because what else can you give men? – and wrapping them up. This exercise always reminds me of the bridal gown – something which is put on only so that it can be taken off – and irritates me to the roots of my being. I really am becoming unhinged on the subject of packaging. I think I see it as prurient, and I hope I'm not inclining towards naturism. The climate is not conducive to unashamed nakedness, and I do not care for the sight of unclad creatures unless they're under eighteen months of age or furry – chimpanzees, chipmunks, dormice etc.

I have myself been unprecedently packaged for a few days. Locked away in exile in a flat with every mod con so I can do some long-delayed work without interruption. There *are* interruptions – the central heating turns itself on with a roar, the electric oven yelps, the extractor thing in the bathroom susurrates, the fridge sighs, but the phone seldom cheeps because few people know where I am, and those that do don't seem to care. There's a blue tit in the berried bush below the window but I don't *have* to bird-watch it, and there's a very busybody dog who ranges round outside unceasingly, looking for something to stick his nose in. I haven't seen him sit down once. I think his owners put him out when they go to work so that he doesn't get upset by the roaring, yelping etc. of the mod cons, and after the day's activity he probably goes straight to sleep the minute they get in.

I'm going back to the house tonight with fourteen pages of MS. I didn't get the letters written, but then I never do. Janet's mended the fuse, and with any luck she'll have been to Waitrose and picked up the mince-pies, red-currant jelly and all the packets of stuff that become necessary at this time. There isn't anywhere to put them because the shelf space is full. We'll have to edge round them until they get eaten up, and then I'm going to run

157

away again: off to the country, I think, where there are dozens of rooms and if anybody gets into a rage he can go and sulk by himself in the west wing. I'm not saying that anybody will. All I'm saying is if I wasn't alone in this wee flat I would eventually murder whoever was with me because I couldn't get away from him. There isn't even a potting shed. I'd never thought of that before. I've always had immediate access to the ground floor without having to fiddle with half a dozen keys. If the need arose I could always sweep out, slamming the door. Here you have to stop and lock several behind you. Easier to clobber the cause of offence and pop him down the waste disposal unit. I can hear the squeak of the mite reminding me to pass on what he told me. He said having a pseudonym was a form of packaging, of disguise, like a wig. He said, 'You're Alice Thomas Somebody Else – so there.'

Mortal coil

The mite who inhabits my unconscious intruded into my waking hour the other morning with a dreadful pun. I had been dreaming about an enormous serpent who was on his way to flatten a castle, and the mite popped up, saying, 'I just coiled to say I love you.' I never say things like that when I'm conscious, I don't even think them. When other people say things like that I pour beer on them.

When the mite returned to his cranny I moved into the

parking space myself and started thinking about suicide. I know it's forbidden, but I wondered whether there might not be circumstances when it's allowable – like when you're about to appear on telly, or Christmas is coming, or somebody expects you to produce 70,000 words by April. There's a certain panache about ritual suicide if you remember the moves correctly, though it can go embarrassingly wrong. Take the Japanese variety. You have to stick a sword in yourself and unravel your insides round it like so much spaghetti. It's not the sort of thing you can practise, and if you make an error a long-suffering friend has to bale you out. Rolling his eyes heavenwards and muttering 'Can't you get anything right', he has to stroll up and swipe your head off. It's asking a lot of friendship.

The third son was in a pub near Beachy Head the other day and asked the barman whether he had many customers hell-bent on self-destruction. 'Yus,' said the barman judiciously, 'I fink we've 'ad fifteen so far this year.' He said you could frequently distinguish them from the normal run of customers who were merely there for the beer. There was something about their expression. The son enquired whether he was not sometimes moved to attempt to prevent them and he said after a moment's contemplation, 'Well, no, not reelly ...' I suppose the bar staff can only take social work so far. The nearby call-box was out of order and the barman said he thought it might have been closed down because people kept using it to deliver their final messages. I just thought that if we all had to rely on British Telecom to relay our last words there'd be people all over the country wondering why on earth we'd done it.

I have a theory about poor Canon Bennett. I couldn't understand why being caught out being rude about the leadership of the C of E should have driven him to take his life. I should rather have expected him to have basked. There are many people of the same opinion as he, and many who would have expressed themselves more cogently. Then when I read that his cat had died in a distressing fashion I began to understand. If he lived alone with it they would have had a close relationship. With the wolves baying at his heels in that maddeningly self-righteous way, and the prospect of further advancement closed to him, finding Kitty laid out on the carpet would be the final straw. We're not supposed to mind about animals as we do about people, but some of us mind, if not more, at least as much. When the fifth son went to Canada he was mildly sad to leave us, but what really upset him was returning his boa-constrictor to the shop because we were loth to look after it. Animals are frequently better company than humans and they don't argue about where the mustard should be positioned on the table. I don't mourn them as I do people, but I remember some pets with such pity and regret. They were sinless – a peculiarly disarming, inhuman quality – and much more straightforward than your average Anglo churchman. I bet they go to Heaven and, as I said earlier, the idea that some suicides might get in with a caution is not perhaps beyond the bounds of possibility.